John Wright Follette's

Golden Grain

Two Trees Ministries

Golden Grain
By John Wright Follette

All Scripture quotations are from the Authorized King James Version of the Bible unless otherwise noted.

ISBN: 978-1514792261

Cover Art: *Harvest*, Volodymyr Orlovsky (1842-1914)
Cover Photo: John Wright Follette, Flower Pentecostal Heritage Center

PUBLISHED BY TWO TREES MINISTRIES, INC.
www.twotreesministries.com
Santa Maria, Ca.

Printed in the United States of America

FOREWORD

By Two Trees Ministries

The last three centuries were a golden age for Christian preaching and teaching and because these eras coincided with the use of the printing press, many great messages were preserved. Some continue to be widely available but others have been left to gather dust on shelves or to mildew in damp basements. As recently as a few years ago if, by chance, a Christian pilgrim happened upon one of these forgotten treasures the cost to re-publish would have made that very difficult. Now, what was once costly and difficult is inexpensive and easy.

Christians living in this the 21st century are replete with messages to hear and to read and yet our hunger for revelations which grow our faith is rarely met. We listen, we read and we study, often not understanding that the gnawing hunger we feel is for the knowledge of Christ, Truth Himself. He is our food and drink and when we find messages centered on Him our faith grows and our spirit sings.

To fill this need, Two Trees Ministries is on the hunt for the forgotten messages of those who followed hard after Christ and were obedient to record their journeys, trials and revelations. And because we can take advantage of this age of digitization, we will offer these works in printed, audio and e-book forms.

At Two Trees Ministries, we are committed to the preservation and accessibility of great preaching and teaching for hungry, fellow pilgrims. We trudge together the narrow way, carrying our cross and in love with the One we follow with all our hearts: Christ.

Santa Maria, California

CONTENTS

INTRODUCTION

I want to help you. I have lived a little longer than some of you, and God has seen good to discipline me, and take me on into the realm of the Spirit, with revelation of light and help. Out of that field, I have made my discoveries, and I want to share them with people— those who are open and desire help. So keep your heart open, and very likely God will drop in a portion of Truth.

I am 80 years old now. When one comes up to this part, one can naturally see he doesn't have a terrific future, fifteen or twenty years ahead of him. I can remember when I used to look 5, 10, 15, 20 years—even 50 years ahead of me, but when one gets to be 80 years old, he doesn't look 20 years ahead. That is past. That doesn't disturb me, because I am now more conscious of the things which are pushing ahead of me into my new age. That is why the things of time don't bother me as they do other people. I am not blaming you if you are disturbed over things of time; you are still related to time; you are thinking of your houses, lands, property, and work. When you have exhausted those things, and you feel your projection is moving into this other realm, you can't come back and be all fuddle-duddled with this.

I am spiritually minded; my feet are upon the earth, but my heart is in heaven. It is good to be in both realms, and to adjust yourself. That is really living.

When I teach, I am teaching out of my heart; not out of a book. I teach out of my life. This gives me authority to preach and teach things I wouldn't otherwise. "Out of the abundance of my heart", I dare to say and do things that I wouldn't if I were teaching theory, or teaching something I read about in someone else's pattern.

He has given me vision, illumination, and discernment in the Word. I can't tell you how I know Truth; I just know. The Holy Spirit in me knows. I can tell Truth the minute I hear it. It took me fifty years to dig it all out and organize it. I can only hope to get you intrigued and hungry so that you will venture in. All I hope to do is try to open the Word.

Teachers are a gift of the Holy Spirit to the Church. I am a disciplined spirit; discipline is my middle name. The Lord had to put me through a lot of schooling. He had to let me go through a lot of things, so that now I know what I am talking about. I don't tell about the tragedies; that is nobody's business. You don't publish your sufferings; you mask them. That is scriptural: "You anoint your head." (Matt. 6:17, 18)

The revelation of God and Truth is very delicate, and fleeting, and sensitive; I can discern it in a person, or a church, or anywhere.

Truth that I give you is not mine; I've discovered it. I am not original in these things at all. I have had training—I don't use that; it's all right in its field—but Truth, you see, doesn't always come that way. Truth is a matter of spiritual revelation, and the process for becoming receptive for the Truth is very terrible. But I mustn't tell you that, because that is so negative! Truth is not mine in its originality. Truth has come to me in these many, long years by patient waiting upon God, and looking, observing, studying, praying, surrendering, dying. A thousand things are united to bring about the technique required for receiving the revelation. So what I have would be Truth which has become possessive in the sense of my own life being held under its power. Truth is never yours; never mine, until it is personalized in our hearts and lives.

I remember the quotation of an old mystic: "The way to heaven is through hell." I believe it. How many are beginning to believe it too? Yes, it's true. God gives us the taste of it—not in all its fullness—the horror of it; the feeling of it, before we are released into the light. We have to go through the darkness in order to appreciate the light. The first reaction to Truth is negative—it will slay us. The second reaction is that it's the only thing God has to quicken us; we have to be slain before we're quickened.

There is no Easter morning, with a resurrection, unless there has been a Friday of crucifixion. We all want the Easter morning, but we can't have our Easter morning in our hearts until we have the tragedy of a Friday. No one wants the ordeal, but that is God's order. I found that even though it was most penetrating, most disastrous, and I suffered tremendously through it, still I said, "Lord, I see that. It's so tremendous that I don't want it any other way."

Can you see how this can be possible? It becomes possible for me, because I begin to sense the fruitage of it, and, though it means going through hell, what I am getting on this side is so tremendous, I'll go through two hells! I don't want to surrender the process, and get it by any other way—that's not legitimate.

Heaven, to me, is to have that strange thing He has awakened in my heart, and has left wounded, tired, and sick, completed in Him.

The power of the Word of God, and the cross of Jesus Christ have been the two instruments that have released me more than anything on God's earth. The revelation of that Word, and the ministry of the cross of Christ, canceling, slaying, but resurrecting into life, have been the most liberating agencies I can give as a testimony of anything that has touched me.

Half the time, I don't live in time here. It's too terrible, but I do live in God; in His Word, which is the Truth. If it were not for the Truth to hold me, I wouldn't be here. That Truth has gripped my heart and life, and has unveiled the Christ to me; unveiled God to me, and helped me to see a little bit of who I am. I don't know yet who I am; maybe I'll find out in some other age. I find all these strange things in and about me that I don't know anything about. How many of us know who we are? How many think we know anything of the essence of what we are; or its light; or its illumination? Very little. We have contact with the Infinite in God through the Holy Spirit, but, as to finding out the essence of this new creature, we are just babes, just little babes coming along, and He wants us to grow.

Aren't you glad for all these people, like Jacob and Peter; that lived before us? They got through, so now I can go through too. I am a normal, natural, human being, but I am a new creature and my emphasis is upon this new creation.

The definition of the word "believe" is: "to adhere to; cleave to Truth; to have faith in an Absolute Person, reliance on the Lord Jesus Christ." He will bring us into a place where no one else can help us.

In a crisis, one time, everybody was trying to tell me what to do, and not one ever helped me. I said, "Lord, why?" He said, "I didn't want them to. They never have the answer." I am glad sometimes God gets us into a place where nobody can counsel us; then we will get to God where we belong! The Word He gave me was in Song of Songs 2:3: "I sat down under His Shadow, (the apple tree) with great delight, and His fruit was sweet to my taste." He told me, "I AM your apple tree."

I think sometimes the reason why I love Him is, because I am conscious of such a reduction of this thing called Follette. I am the most helpless creature who walks the earth; the most dependent creature; that is why I love Him so tremendously. It is because I have nothing to offer Him, but the desperate need in the depths of my being, and I expose it to Him like that. I have nothing to offer. I am silenced. I am learning how to lean.

I am living now more and more with the idea of projection in my praying. How many times I've said, "Lord, I'll never see here what I am praying about." Last year I was very much in intercession and prayer. Sometimes I would stop and say, "Lord, this is terrific praying; I'll never live to see its fulfillment." He said, "You don't need to." The power of prayer penetrates, and pushes on ahead.

I said, "How could I be praying for people and conditions that I will never see?" Do you know what He said to me? He said something sweet. He said, "You look into the 17th chapter of John." There you will find the Lord praying: "Oh Father, I pray not only for these (that's the immediate); I pray for those whom Thou wilt yet (that's in the future) give Me." And God said to me, "The Lord Jesus prayed for you two thousand years before you were born." Did you ever stop to think of that? Jesus prayed for you and me two thousand years before we were born. Then I said,

"You can pray, and intercede through me whatever You want, because I am only an instrument." Isn't it nice to be in touch with an infinite God like that!

I keep living all the time in a projection. I am more concerned with it—its relation to what lies ahead, than with the immediate. That's why it will be wonderful to be released. I haven't a thing here that I would hang on to ten minutes; not at all. I am not morbid, but I sense things, and see through things. My! To be released!

I have a freedom in God—I live detached; free from bondages. If He wants the house—fine! It was His to begin with. I'm detached. Paul said he not only counted the loss of all things, but suffered it. First: Consent. Second: Actual experience.

I am praying all the time; I sing to Him, and pray to Him. Why? Because my heart has found that attitude while I am going about my work. "Pray without ceasing." (1 Thes. 5:17) Prayer is going on all the time in me. Then when I sit at my table, do I say, "Excuse me, Lord, I have to say grace now?" No, that is a religious habit. How many know I am saying grace by the hour!

I don't stay on my knees just to be religious. When the spirit is on me, I pray; if not, I get up and go.

I live all the time by faith, but I'm not conscious it is faith.

I have a God who tells me an awful lot of good things, just lots of them, which I never read in a book.

The Lord and I don't live in a push-button age—it won't work. I am a realist; there is nothing artificial about me.

I live in the Spirit, but my feet are on the earth. I can tell beans from buttons, but at the same time I live with the Lord. I live in the world, but I am not of it. We are to learn to do that—we have to learn a detached life. I live here, but all the time my heart is quite detached.

The Lord saw to it that I have a picture window looking into the mountains. He caters to our weaknesses, idiosyncrasies, and to our temperaments. He knows I am a poet, and an artist, and I do all that business in the aesthetic, or philosophic world. There I am at home, but don't give me an automobile! I would be crazy with it, and mechanical things, and figures. There is something in the realm of art and philosophy, and the aesthetic realm that give me a second youth. I am eighty years old, and I feel as though I were thirty-five. It seems like a hundred years ago since I was a Hebrew and Greek student.

I enjoy the trees and the mountains. I am in love with God's out-of-doors. The whole display of His creative mood in nature is like a holy sacrament. When we are still, the Holy Spirit gives us some interpretation, and intimation of its message.

Those who know me can read between the lines, and sense the basic Truth in all my songs and poetry that God gives me, about life, joy, sorrow, hopes, tragedy, pain, and ecstasy—all make my material.

My poems have plenty of gospel; only served in a little different form. The poetic urge is heavy in me. I didn't make it; I discovered it.

I can feel with a brokenhearted mother; God has made me that way—I can feel with an aged person, or a retarded one. I suffer with them; I feel it all through me.

To me, heaven is a consummation, a sublimation, and a satisfaction of this eternal, terrific urge in my heart for the love of God eternal. And you can have all your heaven and harps etc. . . . . that's good, but that will never satisfy me.

There is something in my heart that is broken, and it will be satisfied only in Him. When I touch that; that's it. He has wounded my heart, and has broken it. There is just no mending, so let it be. He is the Answer, and He has purposely wounded some of us. If He has taken the time to wound your heart, even though it is a distressing thing, love Him anyway, because the sequel to that will be revealed in heaven.

I've nothing in which I am original. I have discovered Truth. I have found it, and have dedicated my life to it. I asked God to make me one who is receptive. I discover the Truth; it isn't mine. I don't sit down and make up Truth. When I discover it, then I ask God to give me the power of transmitting it, releasing it, and giving it out. Then there must be receptivity. The teaching ministry is unique, and different from any other. The Holy Spirit will witness to Truth in us whenever we find it. Build a shelf in your heart for Truth you cannot at present fit into things; don't discard it; in time you will need it.

I have made fresh, little discoveries of Truth; discoveries of how God does things; discoveries of how a human being will act, and react when God does this, and when He does that, and by and by I find out how God works.

John Wright Follette, 1963

CHAPTER I

Baptism of the Holy Spirit is the divine explosion within the innermost part of man which brings to the surface all things good and evil.

If you don't find an interior revolution which will affect the external, I question your experience of the baptism of the Holy Spirit.

1. The Holy Spirit is always the dynamic, the power for any of the things God will do. It was the Holy Spirit working in the Old Testament in every sign and miracle. God is causation; Jesus executes the will; the Holy Spirit accomplishes the work.

2. The baptism in the Holy Spirit is the dynamic by which the mystical Body of Christ can be

formed, and the emphasis of God today, dispensationally, is that of getting His Body ready, shaped up, filled with life, vision, hope, so that He can take her home. That is His great program!

It is time people got acquainted with the objective for which this marvelous, unheard of outpouring was sent!

God's first thought is not what we can do, but what we can become.

Works are subservient to what we become.

Jesus said He would call us out; He would train us; give us discipline; He would give us all that was needed in the way of separation, and light, and illumination, and, most of all, the terrible training which was necessary to conform us into the image and likeness of Himself—the Bridegroom, because we would be the Bride. The Bride must have some features like unto the Bridegroom. He will begin to restore, reshape, repattern, and redesign in us—in this Body with the features that are becoming here, so that someday we may be taken out of this earth, and united with Him, and projected into the things of the eternal ages. For in Ephesians it says that through the Church, He will show His glory and grace in ages to come. This is the instrument. So He says, "Ye shall be unto Me My witness in the world." The power of the Holy Spirit will come upon you, and immerse you into what He is, and Who He is, and YOU will BECOME identified with Him.

". . . Ye shall be witnesses unto Me . . ." (Acts 1:8b) Become this thing: a witness unto God—unto God first. Become unto Me: a process: All Swings to the glory of God. That is the real functioning; that is the ultimate.

"Ye shall become,"—not DO! I believe in works—absolutely. But I want it in its order in God, in the Spirit. He doesn't say a thing we are going to do. He says something that we are becoming; something that we will become. Why? Under the dynamic of this Spirit; He will immerse us under its power. He will not destroy our individuality or our personality concept and fundament of being; He will not do that. He wants every kind, every one of us, but it shall be an immersion—you go out of sight! You go out of sight! You are not sprinkled.

If you ever get the real baptism of the Spirit, the 'you' is lost, your identity, your manifestation—the 'you' is submerged—out of sight. All of that potential of the 'you' that wants to get into prominence, it is out of sight; it is buried; buried! He says, "I will immerse you, I will baptize you in the Spirit and under the impact and power of this dynamic, you shall become unto Me in the world My witness." Why is it that Jesus should say to them on this occasion: "Ye shall become . . ."? It is a verb of being, not of action. However, in order to build this Body, we will find He will give us so many things to occupy us, but all of that is reactionary, the effect; the reaction from the doing reflects right back again to the Body. That is why we contribute to the building of the Body. Becoming is a process. The Holy Spirit was given in that baptism for the building and making of this Body.

Why did Paul pray as he did? Did you ever look at the prayers of Paul? Go into the New Testament and follow all the prayers of Paul and see what the burden of them was. Every last prayer that is mentioned was concerning this Body; it was concerning the believers; it was concerning those who were incorporated in this mystical thing. The burden of prayer on Paul's heart was the completion and the building and making of this Body. What is the burden on the heart of Jesus? The redemption of the world? No. He had died for the world, He can't do any more than that! His prayer in John 17 is, "I pray not for the world, but for them which Thou hast given Me; for they are Thine." The

Holy Spirit is praying "for the saints according to the will of God."

The submerging of the Spirit is the only dynamic by which this Body can be built and brought to completion.

CHAPTER II

THE BRIDE OF CHRIST

Eve was taken OUT of the body of Adam. Notice that it was not the whole body of Adam which made the bride. So, too, out of the Body of Christ can come His Bride. This also is brought about by a separation. He calls the overcoming group His Bride. The whole group, or body, is not the Bride. The highest expression in God's thought, He calls the Bride.

God is using the world to hammer out a Bride. They crucified Jesus. Do you think we are going to have any more glorious ending? Don't worry; we will have to know something of the fellowship of the sufferings and defeat of the Bridegroom. He went home in shame and disgrace, without the applause and satisfaction of the world; He went out in darkness. Do you think the Bride is going home on a bandwagon? A lot of people are trying to get that bandwagon painted up now, so it will play real good.

Where will the Bride—the overcomers—be in this picture? She will be identified with a slain Bridegroom, and the Bride will know something of being slain. The Bride of Christ will know the slain life, and she will go home as a slain Bride in union with the Bridegroom. She comes from the desert, leaning. As long as there is an ounce of flesh, she will stand in her own strength. God has to reduce and deplete her, and bring her to complete exhaustion of self-effort. In Song of Solomon we read: "Who is this that cometh up from the wilderness, leaning upon her beloved?" In Hosea 2:14 it says, ". . . I will allure her, and bring her into the wilderness, and speak comfortably unto her." He charms her and allures her into the wilderness so that He can speak love words to her. It is a love scene; a trysting, so that He might speak love words to her; to have her whole attention; to have her whole heart. Leaning means dependence. We see John at the Last Supper leaning on Jesus' bosom; there is a language between them. Jesus waits for somebody to come near enough to hear His heartbeat—breaking.

In the Song of Solomon, toward the end, the Bride becomes so intense with longing for her

Bridegroom, that she dares to speak. I suppose as we, too, go on with God, we become so bold in our resistance to the world that we become almost offensive to people. They will say: "Where are your interests? Don't you have any touch for the world? Can't you be absorbed in it?" We just say, "We can't. We have none." Our interests are not here. They are over there with Him: The Bride, right in the presence of that King Solomon (the world) declares it, as he turns and describes her beautifully as she really is. He describes her, and the world knows there is something peculiar, because she won't come under the philosophy of this world, but under the philosophy of the Spirit. "Forget thy people;" (human contacts) who have served us. The time comes when God won't let us have a crutch to stand on. HE wants to be the satisfying portion. "Forget thy people"—it doesn't mean we don't like them anymore, but we don't let them have an influence in our life. We become independent of them; released. We keep them in their proper place. "Forget thy people and thy father's house"—a separation as was the case with Rebekah. (Genesis 24) "My father's house" is our natural concept of life; the natural flesh concept.

If we dare to lean, we will hear! He is wooing us again to a mystical union with the eternal heart of God.

The Church is holding us back from the coming of the Lord. "Let us be glad and rejoice, and give honor to Him: for the marriage of the Lamb is come, and His wife hath made herself ready." (Revelation 19:7)

CHAPTER III

CHOICES AND DECISIONS

We are standing here, and we are the sum total of all the choices and decisions we have made in our lives. They have all registered, and this, is the composition of our character. We live in our wills.

We forget, when speaking about heaven, that so many of the things which are for us in the ages yet to come, after this life has been lived, and we as a conscious entity, a spirit released from the body, and moving in the new resurrection body, in a new spiritual realm, most of the things that we have on that other shore—over there in the ages—are DETERMINED HERE.

Now don't think that we can just live a Christian life as happy as bumble bees, and, when we go to heaven, everything is going to be so wonderful. I am sorry to disillusion some people. It isn't going to be that way! Right here and now, we are making the decisions; the choices; the surrenders; the outpourings of life. We are doing that HERE, and THAT WILL DETERMINE what we will have over there. That is not built up all of a sudden over there; not at all. We determine all that right here and now.

Life is too short for us to put into manifestation much that we would choose. Even with a good choice, life is too short for it. But I tell you one thing, life is long enough so that when Truth is presented, and there is an occasion for us to make a decision; or a surrender; or die a death; or accept a Truth—right here is where we do it, but the fruitage, the real fruitage of it, won't always be seen here. We aren't here long enough; the real fruitage will be projected in the things yet to come.

Remember when Jesus was talking about the talents? He said the same thing to all three men; (two were faithful and one wasn't) He said, "Thou hast been faithful over a few things . . . I will now give you a gold house to live in, a pair of wings to fly with, and also a harp!" No, all of those things hadn't anything to do with what He was talking about. He said, "Thou hast been faithful over a few things." What was the reward? A gold crown? A harp? No, the reward was the lifting up of a quality of faithfulness, which the two men earned here, and projecting it upon a new plane over there; multiplied!

The reward was not the material things which most hymn writers put in singing books. The reward for those men was the faithfulness which they had acquired HERE, multiplied and projected upon a new level; on a new plane. Jesus said, "Thou hast been faithful over a few things, you will also now be faithful over many things."

People think that, when we die, God is going to give us all presents; that He is going around with a big clothes basket full of crowns and saying, "Here's a crown . . . and I won't give you any, you missed chapel twice. . .?" He doesn't do any such fantastic things like that in the world. CROWNS ARE WON! We EARN THEM—they are not souvenirs. Crowns are symbolic of certain authority and power which we merit and earn while we are here. It is here that we make our decisions, and certain surrenders. We have to die to a lot of things that nearly kill us—they SHOULD kill us!

The trouble is we don't die. We say, "It nearly killed me." It is supposed to kill us . . . so we will learn.

CHAPTER IV

THE CHURCH

There has always been a main objective towards which every manifestation of God moves. Each dispensation shows this. Today it is the Body of Christ.

What was the burden of Paul's prayers? It was for the growth and development of believers—the Body. It was not bringing in the kingdom and getting this world set straight, nor was this the object of Jesus' prayer. His burden was bringing out of the world as many as possible into salvation. "Go ye to the ends of the earth with the gospel message;" not to Christianize the world, but to evangelize the world. And having evangelized the world, to gather them together in what He calls the Body of Christ. So we should spend our effort and time on this group. This is brought out in Ephesians 4:11-13: "And he gave some apostles; and some, prophets; and some, evangelists; and some, pastors and teachers; For the perfecting of the saints, for the work of the ministry, for the edifying of the Body of Christ; Till we all come in the unity of the faith, and of the knowledge of the Son of God, unto a perfect man, unto the measure of the stature of the fullness of Christ." The Spirit, and even all of the personality gifts relate to the edification of that unique, strange, mystical group of people—the Body of Christ.

I am so glad that all direction is in the Head. Here is my body, He does not expect my hands to be my brains; He expects them to serve what my mind directs. And we forget that Christ is the Head of the Church. Christ is the Head of the Body and, therefore, there should be nothing originating in us; only receptivity to perform and do that which is actuated and directed from the Head. We move around and that is why I think the church or Body is so feeble, because it doesn't know how to live from the Living Head. We try to produce what the Head wants to produce. The Head wants to make the program. He only asks us to function as members, not as the Head!

It takes us a long time to find that out. We are so used to directing from our own natural self; our own head directing what our body is to do, but God says, "No, not that any more. You will become just a member in My Body, for I am the Head." All direction; all programs; anything that is worthwhile at all should originate in Him. He has to have us as a Body through whom He executes and moves. What a burden that would take off of our hearts and lives if we could ever believe it and learn it.

Churches in the book of Revelation have a work complex, instead of a worship complex.

Ephesians 2:21: "In Whom all the building fitly framed together groweth unto an holy temple in the Lord." This verse has to do with the things of God in the holy temple. It has to do with prayer, outpouring intercession, worship, adoration; all that pertains to God. It is all Godward—all that is going on in the temple. He says, "I am building you into a temple; each of you is a stone in the temple, so that ye may be a habitation for God; for all that goes on in the temple." The stones take hours to chip off and hammer, but by and by He fits them into the temple. "You looked like a mountain when I first got you, but this little stone is all you are, and I am fitting you into this temple."

The idea of meeting together in an informal mood—receptivity—is really apostolic. That was the mood, the approach the early disciples had. They had no form. They didn't have singing books with *Jingle Bells* in them! What were they singing? They were singing the Psalms from the Old Testament, and many of the tunes were in minor key under the pattern of the old Jewish synagogue worship. Now that is all they knew, and God recognized it. You see when they came out of Judaism there was nothing formed as a pattern that was left for its development. God never gave any orders as to the form or shape their worship should take. He allowed them to shape it in accordance with what they felt in their hearts to do. The only two ordinances He left us are those of Baptism and the Lord's Supper; these are the only two that He instituted. He didn't institute all the ordinances we have now, but they have come up with the church, because if we don't have anything besides what the Lord instituted we are possessed to have something; so we will invent a form of worship. This isn't wicked or bad, and may be a means of helping some weaker soul towards God. So, I am not too critical, but I don't want that, I don't need it.

In God, and in the Spirit there is originality and spontaneity, but we have lost track of it. I remember in the earliest days of the outpouring of the Spirit that those were the two characteristic marks of the moving of the Spirit—a spontaneity and an originality in His movings. Nothing was programmed or fixed. But you know, when we slip away from that into a stereotyped fashion, the Spirit isn't always pleased to follow us in our little pattern.

Speaking of persecution in the early Church, it was the impact of truth that caused them to move as they did—to take the persecution. It was this strange impact of life that possessed the early Church, and made them different.

The Church was founded on the testimony; not on Peter, but on his testimony of who Jesus was.

There are five personality gifts: apostles, prophets, evangelists, pastors, and teachers. (Eph. 4) He placed them in the Body. Even evangelists, whose ministry is out in the world and darkness, have the Body as a home base for inspiration and direction. For the Body is controlled by The Head. My head has no business planning anything. My head was made to execute what The Head planned. We are the members; we are not The Head, and members of His Body can only serve as The Head directs. Stop shoving evangelists out into the world with artificial objectives such as trying to bring the world to the Lord, clearing up politics, and getting everything in shape. Where did that come from? From religious tradition.

It is so much easier to do something than to become something. So, in the Church, it is easier to do programs and activities than to abide, evolve, and become. God is after the becoming, and so He says, "I have placed all the personality gifts in the Church." Don't project them out into the world. The evangelist functions to the ends of the earth! That's his field— but he has to come back. Why? Because he is getting the material out there to make the Body, and he brings it back into the Body. What is the Body made of? The Body is made of raw material; redeemed humanity. God's emphasis is upon building a Body, and not upon redeeming the world. He has placed the personality gifts there, "FOR the perfecting of the saints, FOR the work of the ministry, FOR the edifying of the Body of Christ."

CHAPTER V

COMMUNION

He is a seeking God—seeking with a broken heart; not getting the response which He should have in the creature. We say our hearts get so hungry, but God's heart is so hungry. When did you give Him anything to satisfy Him? When did you feed Him? The first picture of His broken heart is found in Genesis 3:8-10, and the last one in Revelation 3:20. In Revelation He says, (to an individual; not to a collective group): "Behold, I stand at the door and knock; if any man hear My voice, and open the door, I will come in to him, and will sup with him, and he with Me. I won't coerce you; I won't open the door."

God is coming to that door saying, "Adam, where art thou?" He is saying the same thing, because the same Adam is still dwelling in there; and, in that original thought of God for man, there is still a throbbing Heart longing that we would open to Him, "You were made for Me, and I for you. My heart is aching and longing for you." There will be a restoration of what was lost way back in the Garden; Jesus will restore it in any individual who wants that experience back again.

I asked the Lord about "sup with Him, and he with Me." He said, "I let them always offer to Me first, because I am a Guest, and I will sup with them using whatever they have to offer Me." We bring our resources; we lay it all before Him; we have sweet fellowship with Him, but our resources are soon exhausted. "I let them have the first privilege," our Lord says, "Then I supply Eternal Bread, Eternal Life; all that has eternal value."

What a time we have bringing our little crooked loaf of bread, scorched, and all out of shape. We nearly die trying to get it consecrated to the Lord, but He says, "I take it, dear, and I have a Loaf too; partake of it forever!"

A Communion Prayer:

We are all so self-centered about our comings and our goings, our little lives, our little doings, and our fussing around. Dear Lord, help us to get away from that. Let our inner beings pour out to Thee in a holy, loving consecration, a surrender, and a yielding of all that we have. Let it flow back again to Thy loving heart. Teach us how to enter into communion with Thee; deliver us from prayer patterns, and help us to be normal, natural, and real with Thee so that Thou wilt be able to receive from us that which would satisfy and please Thy heart.

CHAPTER VI

THE CROSS

Every man will find his discipline, and every man will find his cross. All Christians are not disciples. When He first introduces the cross, it is to Christians. Jesus Christ never places a cross on anybody. It is in our volitional power of will to choose. He doesn't lay a cross on us "so we can love Him!" No, we voluntarily take it. He never imposes it; it will be the instrument on which we will be slain. Our cross will be the most liberating thing in our life. As with Christ's cross, it liberates and sets free everything in salvation, and the things of God.

If we want to sidestep the cross and miss its ministries, we won't go to hell, but, if we sidestep this cross, we will sidestep one of the greatest agencies in the economy of God to bring us into God. He says,

"Come, take up this cross as a voluntary act." The cross is the instrument of death, but it brings a fuller revelation to our hearts and lives than that of any other agency in His economy.

If we would know fellowship in the future, we must know it now. We must know the cross in its twofold teaching; not only sins forgiven, but, on the other side, joy: agony—but joy. Embrace it; hang on to it; cruel and bitter though it is; for joy and a sensing of God, as never before, will follow.

Be willing for the crucifixion, because it is the author of LIFE.

The more spiritually minded we are in heart and life, the more we can understand the revelation of God, and the more we understand the cross.

"Though He were a Son," He learned obedience continually. (Heb. 2:10; 5:8) That was like a cross. Learning obedience is a cross which we will have too, if we want to follow Him. "If any man wants to follow Me (to My destiny), let him take up his own cross and follow Me." But this is not the cross which He lays on us; it is something that we may voluntarily resist or accept. It is a cross distinct from trials and testings that He brings upon us. It does amount to great suffering, but it is a suffering in which we have the power to resist if we don't want to take it. Sometimes, for example, great teaching, a great revelation, amounts to a cross. We know if we take that cross up, if we embrace that Truth, if we dare to subject ourselves under the impact and power of that Truth, it is going to be a terrific cross that will kill us. It will crucify us. Well, it is supposed to! Take up YOUR cross.

Your cross and my cross will vary according to the disposition, and the calling of our lives, so we don't have the same in that sense, but everyone will have one.

Why? Because in God's economy and purpose for us, He knows the pattern, the situation, the episode that will perfectly crucify our old flesh. So He says: "Will you voluntarily take it? You pick it up. You know what My cross did for Me. It was the place of My execution; it was the place where I died; now, you take yours. It will be the place of the execution of the creature that you are; it will slay you. I don't lay it upon you; I want you to voluntarily take it up, for then your identification with Me will be what I want— a voluntary love and surrender."

So, He will bring a cross to you; it may take different shapes and forms, but it is always a cross. I can't interpret your cross; nobody but you can. So when God brings it, don't be amazed, upset, and confused.

He says, "Take it up." For if you take up your cross; this decision, this consideration, this surrender; if you take that up into your life pattern and walk, you will have a crown over there. Because the sequel, the answer, to a cross is a crown. And there is no crown without a cross, because every cross, if borne, will take a crown.

"Hold that fast which thou hast . . ." What do we have? We have the Truth, which becomes a cross, which will slay every one of us. Hold fast to the Truth as to a treasure, lest something come along, and snatch it away. Hold fast the Word of Truth which is a cross; it will eventually spell a crown. Snatch your crown! For the crown is the answer to the Truth. Hold to your Truth; hold to your cross; lest in not holding it, the crown is affected.

What is the symbol of suffering? It is the cross.

Christ had His cross every day, and Calvary was the climax. "He was made perfect through suffering." Ready for supreme sacrifice, suffering had done the silent, sacred ministry. ". . . Who for the joy that was set before Him, endured the cross . . ." (Heb. 12:2).

". . . Our light affliction which is but for a moment, worketh for us a far more exceeding and eternal weight of glory." (2 Cor. 4:17) He has gone, but He left His cross. Every man has his own cross to bear, but the sequel is life and secret joy— the crown.

Your cross is your crown in disguise.

Prayer: May we interpret the cross, the crown, the Truth.

CHAPTER VII

DIVINE ARRANGEMENT

A divine arrangement is a certain method or rule by which God works. Never ask Him to change to accommodate your mind; adapt yourself to His method.

2 Timothy 1:7: "For God hath not given us the spirit of fear, but of power, and of love, and of a sound mind." Sound mind is a bad translation; a better one is disciplined spirit. God says, to build this strange, mystical thing—the new man—"I will give you, first of all, POWER, then love and a sound mind (disciplined spirit.)" Now, why did He begin with power? Because power is the dynamic by which the whole thing is made manifest. No need messing around trying to get love or something else. The whole thing is based on a dynamic power God furnishes, which is the Holy

Spirit. You will find the same order in the Old and New Testament, and in your heart and mine. Whenever you see an arrangement like that in the Bible, leave it the way it is written. Some would put love first, instead of power, but we can't change it. There is a divine order.

From creation on, everything that we have comes through the power of the Spirit: (In the Old Testament the word is *ruach*, and in the New Testament it is *pneuma*). They both have the same idea of breath or life—the outbreathing, *ruach*; the breath of God—that is Spirit; that is Life; *pneuma*, breath—pneumonia, pneumatic tire, air, breath, spirit; all come from the same word.

Why do we have the breath of Life? Because we can't receive anything in creation without it. We have it in the life of Jesus. He was conceived by the Spirit; born of the Spirit; baptized in the Spirit; He ministered in the Spirit. His whole life moved in the power of God, called the Holy Spirit, and He lived in it, moved in it, ministered in it; and even when He died, the resurrection was by the Eternal Spirit. If all that was needed in the life of Jesus, how much more we need the power of the Spirit in our lives! We can't get anywhere without the Holy Spirit.

Notice the divine arrangement of the Beatitudes: Never recast them; never change their order. They say, "'Blessed is he, Blessed is he', etc. so why not have them any which way, because they all begin 'Blessed' don't they?" We cannot do that; we have to have a sequence. They HAVE to begin with "Blessed are the poor in spirit," as the basis for all the other "Blessed's" to follow; we cannot change that.

The Sermon on the Mount covers Matthew, Chapters 5, 6, 7. Oh, the Sermon on the Mount! The logic in there is just beautiful! Jesus is teaching His disciples. The whole Sermon on the Mount hasn't anything to do with the sinner at all.

What is the first Beatitude? Does it say those who hunger and thirst after righteousness shall be filled because we have to be hungry first, and we know that is the great basic need? No, that isn't the first Beatitude. The first one begins with a very wonderful statement:

(1)   "Blessed are the poor in spirit; for theirs is the kingdom of heaven."

There could not have been a broader, more beautiful statement. Why? In Greek "the poor in spirit," means "bankruptcy". Blessed—or most fortunate; or, to be envied is better—is a person who has been reduced to bankruptcy, without any potential of his own, for in his bankruptcy, all heaven is his!

Why is there not more heaven in some people? The rich young ruler in Matthew 19, turned away sorrowful, because he had great possessions. Anyone who has great possessions is not going to get too far with the Lord. Most fortunate, to be envied, is a person who is reduced to bankruptcy in any self-resources. "In me dwelleth no good thing." This is basic, because then it is possible for all heaven to be yours. Then Jesus goes on with the rest of the Beatitudes, because they are divinely arranged—in sequence. One makes it possible for the second, and we can't get to the third until we have had the first and second. The point is; their blessedness all runs into a series sequence.

(2)   "Blessed are they that mourn; for they shall be comforted."

Why is this one next? Because the clearer our vision is of Jesus, and the beauty of His loveliness and purity, grace and strength, the more we are truly able to mourn in the true sense of the word—mourn our sin; mourn the nature and cause; mourn because we grieve Him. Then we are comforted by His grace.

(3)   "Blessed are the meek; for they shall inherit the earth."

Whence does this meekness come? What causes our mourning? The Holy Spirit, working in the heart, now produces meekness and brokenness not formerly known to the humanity at all. It is the natural result of this poverty and mourning, which results in grace and comfort. This poverty and mourning produces a meekness in our nature like Christ's. Thus the meek inherit all things—the earth. They are not seeking now; are not proud or lifted up, so He can trust the meek and they are safe. All this has revealed to them their deep need. Now comes the hunger.

(4)   "Blessed are they who do hunger and thirst after righteousness; for they shall be filled."

We have to be conditioned continually in heart and spirit for the reception of that which we hope and long for. Whence this hunger and thirst? Is it for salvation? No. It is for a fuller and fuller revelation of Jesus. God creates the appetite, and fills it from His side. The new creature needs to be fed. "He shall be filled," completely satisfied.

(5)   "Blessed are the merciful; for they shall obtain mercy."

Man, by nature, is not merciful. The Spirit has manifested God's mercy in such measure that man, in turn, becomes merciful himself, and also obtains mercy. "For with what judgment ye judge, ye shall be judged; and with what measure ye mete, it shall be measured to you again." (Matthew 7:2)

(6)   "Blessed are the pure in heart; for they shall see God."

The Spirit is bringing the soul to purity—not sinless perfection, nor faultlessness. The surrendered will—a heart whose only and every motive is Godward is pure in heart. "With the pure thou wilt show Thyself pure." (Psalm 18:26) "With the pure all things are pure." (Titus 1:15) What or Whom do they see? GOD; not only in heaven, but here in everything which touches the life—God first. (Romans 8:28)

(7)   "Blessed are the peacemakers; for they shall be called the children of God."

We are now so united and blessed in fellowship that we enter into the service of the King. He can now truly trust us. (2 Corinthians 5:18-21), (Colossians 1:20.)

(8)　　"Blessed are they which are persecuted for righteousness sake: for theirs is the kingdom of heaven."

This is the natural outcome of life or service in God. We are not of the world; it hates us. "Through much tribulation, and patience ye shall enter the kingdom of God." (Acts 14:22b) "Yea, and all that will live godly in Christ Jesus shall suffer persecution." (2 Tim. 3:12) Suffering is our lot, but all heaven is ours. This is general suffering for the cause of Christ and righteousness in the earth, such as persecutions, involving name, reputation, and principles of Truth for which we become martyrs.

(9)　　"Blessed are ye, when men shall revile you, and persecute you, and shall say all manner of evil against you falsely, for My sake. Rejoice and be exceedingly glad; for great is your reward in heaven; for so persecuted they the prophets who were before you."

What suffering is this? The previous sufferings are general ones; now they will become specific. They will bring you into closer union and identification with Christ, and bring your heart into the "fellowship of His sufferings." (Philippians 3:10, and Colossians 1:24) The climax of the Beatitudes is marked by suffering. It is the desired end.

Let us note two things in the study of the Beatitudes:

1.   The progression and perfect movement or growth; there is sequence of marked significance. One Beatitude grows, evolves, naturally out of the other. There is maturity and growth in strength as the soul is led onward.

2.   It takes the work of the Holy Spirit to produce each step. He alone can bring us, and hold us in each of these positions, for each condition, pronounced "blessed" or "happy", is diametrically opposed to everything natural.

Almost the first revelation which comes to the Christian early in the way is his poverty and lack of spirit. The human spirit is wild, beastlike. Our human spirit breaks down, and cannot work in the new maimed condition into which He has now brought us. Man does not like to be reduced to a "beggar", but only then can the Power of heaven manifest itself. Then Christ can be all in all.

When Jesus was teaching concerning prayer, He gave us three orderly phases of our prayer life: asking, seeking, knocking. Matthew 7:7: "Ask and it shall be given you; seek, and ye shall find; knock, and it shall be opened unto you." Now we cannot disarrange that.

We would spoil the whole sequence; we would spoil the whole arrangement. We do not receive first by knocking; first is the aspect of asking—we ask, and then we receive. Our knocking is the last part. There is something in between —seeking: "Seek and ye shall find."

First comes the spirit; then soul; then body. ". . . and I pray God your whole spirit and soul and body be preserved blameless unto the coming of our Lord Jesus Christ." (1 Thes. 5:23)

Another divine arrangement is found in Psalm 27:1: "The Lord is my light and my salvation; whom shall I fear? The Lord is the strength of my life; of whom shall I be afraid?" Here David is getting his experience in God. What is the first thing he finds?

1. Light. We must have that to get the whole thing going.

2. Salvation.

3. Strength of life.

The full swing of a conception of God is always in a Trinity.

"He is my light." Light dispels darkness, but it also reveals my condition. David is in the realm of darkness, so light must come first. Jehovah God is my light; God, in the beginning, was the Author of it. The Lord is first unto me light. Now the reason for this is that the natural man is born in darkness. God's first approach is light; by that He begins to reveal to us what we are, who we are, and the condition in which we are in.

"He is my salvation." The next bit of revelation is what God will be to David. The Lord is my light, and the Lord . . . is my salvation, my deliverance out of this chaos. So the second phase of this work is the presentation of the Christ in His redemptive work— that of my salvation.

"He is the strength of my life." He is my light— the One Who brings light to me, He is my salvation, delivering me out of my darkness, transforming me into the kingdom of light. Now I find that even here I cannot live it, only in Him. He has to be the very strength of my life. The Holy Spirit is the power and strength of my life. Therefore, in the last analysis, if your revelation of God is perfect, in the sense of completion, it will be a Trinity. David has had a revelation of God. He says, God is a Trinity!

God is my Light—That's the Father. God is my Salvation—That's the Son. God is the Strength of my life— That's the Holy Spirit. No revelation is complete unless it has the Trinity in it. There is a special ministry in my being for each Member of the Trinity. My fellowship is with the Father, with the Son, and with the Holy Ghost.

CHAPTER VIII

DIVINE REVELATION

Never approach the Word as you would approach any other literature. The Holy Spirit is needed for its revelation.

Truth cometh by revelation, and that by the Spirit of God; not by our mental processes, but by the Holy Spirit, Who reveals the things of God to us. (1 Cor. 2:10)

Teachers are those who have gotten into the Word, move in the Spirit, and have revelation, light, and Truth from God by the Holy Ghost. I have the Bible, and I have the Holy Spirit, but they run parallel in their responses. Just as soon as I move in the Word of God, I have to move into a broader, and more glorious revelation of the Lord Jesus Christ.

Jesus said, "I am the Truth." This means that all Truth is personified in Him; all Truth becomes articulate; all Truth becomes fully expressive in this dynamic, marvelous, living Christ, and the nearer we get to Him, the more we love Him. Oh, those profound unfoldings by the Spirit, Who takes us into the Person of Christ, in Whom are hidden the treasures!

If the Holy Spirit has been gracious enough to take us into the darkness, and has said: "Look, you have made a discovery," we come out enriched, because we have found some little, simple treasure in the personality setup of Christ.

There is much that we can have which is quite visible and tangible; what we call the articulate aspect of Him. But there is so much of Him which is evasive. It is abstract, but it is in Christ, and that is where I get blessed. When Jesus was here, He said, "I am the Truth." He means by that: all Truth is summed up in this revelation. "He that hath seen Me, hath seen the Father."

You see, He is talking about a manifestation of the nature and character of God.

The people who gathered about Him, and heard Him speak, saw His manifestation in miracle power.

They were recipients of His grace, and even of His healing, but how many of you think they had any inner revelation as to His identity? No, they didn't; even His disciples did not.

It took Him three years of intensive work for the disciples to even recognize that He was the Messiah, let alone the Son of God! That never entered their brains when they first started out with Him, It was a long time before they even found out He was the Son of God. They all supposed Him to be the son of Joseph. Later on they perceived by His learned exposition, and, finally, through His works, miracle working, and all the rest, that this Man did not teach or speak like any of the rest of them. Well, of course not!

Finally, after three years, they could accept Him as their Messiah, but that is as far as their acceptance went! When Jesus came down from Caesarea Philippi, He turned to His disciples, when alone with them, and asked, "Whom do men say that I am?" Now if He had been revealed in a long white robe with a halo in the back of Him, do you think He would have asked that? NO. Then He asked, "Whom say ye that I am?" He pins them down, He doesn't want a general opinion from them. Peter answered: "Thou art the Christ." (Christ means the Messiah). But he says something more, "The Son of the living God." "And Jesus answered and said unto him, Blessed art thou, Simon Bar-jona for flesh and blood hath not revealed it unto thee, but My Father, Who is in heaven." (Matthew 16:17) This was a revelation by God the Father. Truth comes by a revelation of the Spirit, not by reasoning, logic, scientific deduction, philosophy or any other scheme.

"No man knoweth the Son, but the Father." (Matthew 11:27). Then it takes the Father, through the Holy Spirit, to reveal Him to us, but the Father is really the only One Who knows Him.

Jesus Christ, and the Word of Life run parallel. If we are studying the Word of God as Truth, we will have to have the parallel revelation of the Lord Jesus running with it. Jesus doesn't stand over there, static, as we study something in the Word here. We have to have an inner, personal fellowship with the Lord running parallel with the Word, or there is no life or Spirit in the Word at all. We may have wonderful insight as to the letter of the Word, but there is no corresponding insight into the Lord. We do not have an inner consciousness of entity; no awakening. Anyone who is finding Truth in these deeper, fuller revelations of life in the Word of God, who is still entertaining the same vision and conception of Jesus he had fifteen years ago, is not very far along in spiritual growth. Why? The revelation of Christ, the personality of Christ, must unfold, and unfold, and unfold until we begin to find the treasures of this revelation; TRUTH HIDDEN IN THE CHRIST. It is hidden. Where will we get this Truth? It comes only by a parallel revelation. I never can read that Word of God, and get anything unless there is a continual, parallel revelation all the time in my spirit. I am discerning something new in Him. I see Him in some new slant of light. Why? As I read the Word, I see Him! He's the WORD! Keep that parallel. Don't try to divorce the Lord from the Word.

Keep your parallel: The opening of the Word of God under the power of the Spirit, and the opening as to this wonderful Christ—God—the Eternal Son. God, coming to us in flesh, going home, but coming again in the power of the Spirit. Keep that, all the while, in parallel with the Word. It is a double revelation, and it is sweet, and we should have it!

CHAPTER IX

EMOTIONS

Sometimes I have a test of faith as I mature in God. He doesn't ask me to understand Him, but He understands me perfectly. I don't always understand Him, but I love Him anyway. Sometimes He is very difficult to understand, and I say, "Lord don't look at my tears. Please, look at me, in here, where I'm saying, Yes, Lord. Yes, Lord."

The Lord has a right to leave me without a touch of His Presence for weeks or months at a time. I have my contact without my emotional reaction. If He wants to leave for China for three months, it's all right if I don't get blessed in three months, or even sing a little song while at home walking around. I pay a price for every last thing I get from God. I pay a price for it, and I want to. He is not going to baby me. We have to learn that, and that isn't pleasant. But God is doing something inside of me like a tornado. Then out of that I come out with: "The Lord is wonderful! He IS wonderful!"

The further we go on in God, the less He is going to honor that field of the emotions. We have to learn to walk with the Lord without His conscious Presence, which is very terrifying. Less and less are we dependent on our old devotional patterns that served for our living. How can faith develop if He is going to humor us along all the time?

In those difficult places we will never be able to synchronize the state in which we are moving with our fluctuating emotions. They will not always flow together. We are trying to let our emotions run parallel with our experience.

CHAPTER X

END TIME

All the fields will be going into distortion—music, philosophy, literature, everything. The enemy comes in to distort it—the rhythm and beauty are gone. We see it in every field. The standards that maintained, and were good in their own fields, that all is undermined; in the nations, in government, in schools, in family life. God will let it run on that mechanism until it will run out on that. It is antichrist contrasting against Christ; against Truth; and a spirit of lowliness: May we be able to discern, and distinguish between them.

People call the confusion and thunder in the nations today, a roar. It is a roar, but I hear God; I hear GOD; I HEAR GOD! When people are saying, "the roar" today, I hear the roar, but I also hear the voice of God, and He is speaking to those whose ears are attuned to Him, so they will not "think it strange." "What do you hear?" they ask. Well, you wouldn't believe what I hear, but I am not the only one. I have friends around the world, and I say to them, "Do you hear it, dear?" And they say, "Yes, it's an indication that it is God; it is God speaking; the movings of God." All some hear are the signs of the times, and the war, and some other things.

I feel that there is an invasion of God all the time. I feel it in the world; I feel like He is pushing in all the time. I feel that toward the end of this time, heaven is pushing toward the earth in its last struggle. I feel it in my spirit; that invasion; that push; that holy urge of God. Some spirits become conscious of it, and are quite overwhelmed with it. They should be. Others are not, and I am very charitable with them.

Prayer:

In these closing days, it seems we need Thee all the more, because we are conscious of the moving of the power of the enemy in every form that he can move in. He is pressing in upon us; he is pressing in upon the whole civilization in every field; the whole order. We are conscious of it. Lord, may we be hidden away in Thee continually, and able to partake of Thee and Thy life and vision enough to stand; to please and satisfy Thee.

CHAPTER XI

FAITH

When God speaks the Word, it has two definite qualities. It is authoritative, and it has creative power. The Word is quickened by the Spirit. Faith lays hold of, and wraps itself around that Word. It is our garrison of strength, and security for faith. Its creative power ministers to our faith and strengthens it.

When He speaks a Word, it has:

1. All the authority of heaven back of it.

2. It is creative.

A grain of faith always goes with the Word. When He gives the Word, He gives faith with it to encourage us.

I don't want a God that I understand. I have a God Whom I can trust where I can't understand. He keeps much in the background SO that "we walk by faith and not by sight." So I won't understand every last thing. If you would understand God perfectly, there would be no place for faith, and He wouldn't be God.

Truth has to pass the assent of the intellect, and has to come down to the heart. Anyone, who is truly converted to God, is intellectually converted first before his heart is truly converted, for the heart must have that before it is converted with faith. The heart; the whole emotional life, with the will, has taken hold of that Truth. My mind has grasped it long ago; my mind gave assent to it; then it goes to the spirit. It comes down into my inner being. Before the heart can reach out, it has to have an object. Faith demands an object which it can grasp.

CHAPTER XII

FELLOWSHIP

Sometimes, just the offering of our humanity pleases Him. He loved the disciples' presence, but there was failure on their part on the Mount of Transfiguration. They also failed in the Garden, because of their limited spiritual comprehension. Matthew 26:43, "And He came and found them asleep again: for their eyes were heavy." The actual translation here is: "For sheer sorrow they slept. . ."

Degrees of Fellowship

He will give according to the capacity that is opened to Him. There is such a thing as putting that capacity; that receptivity in the hands of God, in the Spirit, so that He can take its potential, and open it until it comes to the fullness of all that God expects. He doesn't expect me to be Peter or Paul. He wants me to be just the creature that I am. He wants you to be just exactly who you are—not trying to strain, or be discouraged because you can't offer to Him what these magnificent saints have been able to offer. Don't be disturbed over that, but be very sure, dead sure, that what opening there is; what capacity you have; that it's surrendered to the Lord all the time. Keep it open all the time to the Spirit; exposed to Him, so that as you read, as you come and as you go, as you speak, preach, sing, or pray, whatever you do, you are exposed there to receive whatever God has to offer. Then He will build up our fellowship. He will strengthen it; He will enlarge it until, when He fills that capacity, you will be just as blessed, and happy, and just as satisfying and pleasing to God as the one who has the capacity of Paul. You can give to God all that He expects of the pleasure and satisfaction from you. So can I. So could Paul. So I call this degrees of fellowship.

We talk about "the fall of man", but the, word "fall" is not mentioned in the Bible—"death is. . . . In the day that thou eatest thereof thou shalt surely die" (Gen. 2:17) Do you think death was in the heart of God when He created Adam? No. When God came, after Adam had sinned, He still had access to him; He still had communion with him. All of his wreckage does not hinder God coming and bringing him out of his wreckage into a glorious new creature, a thing that has never lived on the earth before.

The first picture of a brokenhearted God is here in Genesis when He says, "Oh, Adam, where art thou?" He did not come to rebuke him, but He came to salvage him, and to bring him through. He didn't come down as a Judge, but as LORD God, Who would bring redemption to this whole chaotic being; the whole world. That was the lovely, marvelous Son of God! I want you to love Him.

I only can feel a pathos in God's voice. "Adam, where art thou?" Adam had been made to bring to God a peculiar pleasure that no other thing in the universe could bring. No angels could bring it; no created thing could bring it; but man, in his response, because he is created in the image and likeness of God; could offer back to God that which the heart of God had always hungered for.

He cares about a fellowship with you, more than anything on God's earth. He cares more about the fellowship of your heart than He does anything in the world, because it is something that only YOU can give. People can do so many things. He wants you to become something. There is a process in becoming. Even in the next age I expect to grow. It's merely the releasing of the little seed plot here; the little potential. It took years to get it in shape to be released, and projected to the eternal ages as a media for the glory of God, and to give His heart pleasure. That's what life is about. That's what I want people to see.

After a meeting, I was walking down a lane alone, thanking the Lord, and loving Him. How many ever just love the Lord?

CHAPTER XIII

FLESH

God didn't even want the smell of sweat on the Priests. Anything of the human; the agitation of the flesh; the effort of flesh; He does not want. (Ezek. 44:18)

Do not let the old nature which is still alive, direct traffic—deny yourself.

The Book of Revelation was given to the Church; not the world. Keeping this in mind, God's judgment is coming upon all the earth—our humanity. He is coming to test us and prove us on the flesh level.

CHAPTER XIV

GIFTS

In Romans 11:29 we read that "The gifts and calling of God are without repentance." A gift can be operated purely in the flesh or psyche; it depends purely upon who is back of the motivating and directing. In 1 Corinthians, chapters 12-14 we find Paul correcting their motives regarding the gifts. In chapter twelve he enumerates the gifts (the manifestation gifts as well as the personality gifts); in chapter thirteen he talks of motives back of the gifts; and in the fourteenth chapter he encourages them to seek after the best gifts.

To better understand Paul in his teaching here, we must go back into the original Greek writings where we find that the translators (who are not inspired) have unfortunately placed the first verse of chapter thirteen as the last verse of chapter twelve. Let us read it as it should have been:

"But covet earnestly the best gifts; and yet show I unto you a more excellent way. Though I speak with the tongues of men and of angels, and have not charity (love), I am become as sounding brass, or a tinkling cymbal." Paul is now no longer speaking of the gifts but of a WAY. The Corinthians had all the gifts and all the power. Paul had to correct them, for their motivation was wrong. Rather than their motive coming from their natural heart and life and disposition, it must come from the love of God shed abroad in their hearts and lives; the 'agape' love is to control the power of the manifestation in the gifts. When the gifts are not motivated by the love of God— that broken bleeding heart of Jesus—, if we don't have that to become the motive for their manifestation, it is nothing to God but sounding cymbals and rattles! He warns them that even though the gift may bless somebody, as far as its reaction in the one possessing the gift is concerned, it is not to the glory of God, and the heart is not refreshed, neither does he grow. "It profiteth me nothing."

Paul tells them concerning spiritual gifts, as we read in chapter twelve, that he wants to do a little corrective teaching. He then goes on in chapter thirteen to give the law by which these gifts are to be operated. "Now show I unto you a more excellent way,"—not a more excellent gift. Love is never a gift; love is a fruit. He then goes on to correct their motivation. We will never understand chapters twelve through fourteen of 1 Corinthians unless we read them all as one thing.

CHAPTER XV

GOD

If God wants to appear in a body, He can, but in essence He is Spirit; not a spirit, but He is Spirit. The article is not in the original at all. He is Spirit. That is why He is present everywhere.

I don't define God: I experience Him. I can have a doctrinal idea of God, but afterward I find the reality when I come in touch with HIM.

CHAPTER XVI

GOD'S OBJECTIVE

Prayer:

Thou hast always taken the initiative to reach us. In just that simple, and humble way, we come back and say, "Thank You, Lord; continue to draw us that we may run after Thee and find Thee." We are on our way back to Thy wonderful and loving heart, and we must be prepared to live, and move with Thee. Thou hast given us instruction in the Word, and Thou hast told us the objective that Thou art aiming at; the purpose Thou hast in Thy heart; the desires that are in Thy heart and mind. We want to discover them, and learn how to intelligently cooperate with Thee; to move with Thee under the inspiration of Thy Spirit and leadership.

MY objective is to glorify God. HIS objective is to conform me to the image of His Son. Man was made to glorify God. "Thou art worthy; O Lord, to receive glory and honor and power; for Thou hast Created all things, and for Thy pleasure they are and were created." (Rev. 4:11) "Whether, therefore, ye eat, or drink, or whatsoever ye do, do all to the glory of God." (1 Cor. 10:31)

The glory of God becomes the focal point toward which I move as a Christian. I am doing this for the glory of God. What is your objective for living? The naked will of God is the means to glorify God. "The heavens declare the glory of God." Why? Because the will of God is being done there. God wants people dedicated in every vocation of life. If you are selling neckties, the fact that God's will is being done, glorifies Him. God's will: want it has a holy thing; as a holy trust, whatever it is.

Eph. 2:10: "God has made us what we are, creating us in Christ Jesus for the good deeds which are prepared beforehand by God as our sphere of action." (Moffatt)

Col. 1:16: "For by Him were all things created, that are in heaven, and that are in earth, visible and invisible, whether they be thrones, or dominions, or principalities, or powers: all things were created by Him, and for Him."

Heb. 13:21: "Make you perfect in every good work to do His will, working in you that which is well pleasing in His sight, through Jesus Christ: to Whom be glory for ever and ever. Amen."

Psa. 27:4: "One thing have I desired of the Lord, that will I seek after: that I may dwell in the house of the Lord all the days of my life, to behold the beauty of the Lord and to inquire in His temple."

He didn't make us because He needed us. He made us because of two reasons:

1.   To glorify Him.

2.   To do His pleasure and to do His will.

He gives grace and strength for the execution of His will, and if people will take a little time just to find out His will, it would glorify Him, and we would go leaps and bounds in the things of God. We have a moral and spiritual likeness to God. These are qualities not found in the lower creation. To man He says, "Here is the world; have dominion . . . bring it into subjection so it can serve you, and it will provide all your needs."

I wish you could get the reaction that is in my heart when I look at your hungry hearts. It thrills me. It thrills me to know there are some people in this busy, wild, furious, rat race of a world who still are conscious there is God somewhere: "Where is He? Will somebody help me find Him?" That's what I want too. I want to let God do the work that so many people are trying to do.

Our preachers, and people are so busy trying to help God along, but we don't have to help poor God along. It's all I can do, with what little vision I have, to keep up with Him! What a strange philosophy has bewitched the people! It has bewitched them. God does not need us in that sense. He wants to love us, and He wants us to love Him. When we have a philosophy reduced to such simplicity, we just sit down and say, "Is that all?" He says, "Yes." If we love God perfectly, and we are conscious of His love filling us, we do all the things that are necessary.

Now, wouldn't that take a burden off of ten thousand workers! They bear an assumed burden. I am not saying they are not burdened. There is a difference between a burden we assume—a religiosity, and a burden which HE brings, which is easy. It is light, and there is a sweet consciousness of that undergirding all the while we are carrying it.

He would be greatly helped if He could get some souls aroused, and awakened so that they would love Him, walk with Him, talk with Him, and live with Him. But you see, that reduces life to such simplicity, and our world seems to love complication; multiplied complications, which makes them feel they are going somewhere in the world. But what is their objective? GOD is our objective.

When the sound of God is in a meeting, how many know your heart knows it right away. That's a hangover of creation in its loveliness when it was real in the beginning. Everything was fresh and untouched; undimmed. The response in Adam to God was instantaneous. God could come down and communicate with him, and discuss the things that were on His heart, show him His will, how to possess; how to reclaim the earth. That was all in the heart of God.

Man could respond when God came down in the cool of the evening, through a consciousness, (translated "sound"; or in English "voice") when God hadn't spoken yet. God had not spoken, yet they could hear Him. It's that subtle, strange, mystical union that we have with God—a fellowship that doesn't need words. How many know the closest, the loveliest things we have had in God cannot be put in words? There is a joy; there is glory; there is a deep inner consciousness that no words can tell; that sweetness; that inner communion; how many know it is past words? My deepest prayers have never been words; they are past words.

God always moves toward two striking objectives in His creation: His glory, and His pleasure. These are the two great objectives toward which life is focused. No one claims to be original in God today; this age won't let you say, "Lord, what do YOU want?" Why were we made? I am sure we weren't made for the objective most people have today. "The heavens declare the glory." What are the heavens doing? They are doing the thing for which God made them. Even in inanimate creation, the first objective is "The heavens declare the GLORY of God." Even though creation is under an awful bondage, it still breaks through, and there is glory. How can we glorify God? Wherever the will of God is executed, He is glorified. Do what the Lord tells you to do.

He told Adam, "Have dominion and authority, and cause nature to respond, and all these secrets that are now hidden, will be divulged to you. They will come to you as you grow with Me, and as I release them, and you are built to receive them, you can govern, possess, and move . . ." That was His program.

So He comes and deals with Adam. Adam gave Him great joy, and pleasure, and His creation functioned in the method, and procedure that it should follow. God rejoiced because He was finding satisfaction. God was being glorified.

Then came the temptation. Now temptations are always of the devil. Testings, and provings are always of God. God never tempts us. God proves us, and tests us unto strengthening; unto growth. All growth is under a law of testing and proving.

God had been absent in the interim when Adam sinned. Now, His first coming back, His first contact, is with a dead man with a moral and spiritual nakedness. "They hear the voice of God walking." They were acute to catch the sound which accompanies the Presence of God; the sound which is indicative of His moving. It must have been terrible when He came down, and walked in the cool of the evening, and found no response. Have you ever lost a very dear friend? Isn't it heartbreaking?—Lost—We can't fix it, and we can't mend it; we want to talk, and there is no voice.

God walked the earth to gain a little fellowship from His own creation; to have the understanding, and the mutual intercourse of spiritual life with Adam. Oh, the broken heart of God! We will know it, sometimes, if we ever fellowship with Jesus in all the fullness. How many know it enlarges our whole capacity for God, and I praise Him for every heartbreak. "Farther on, the way grows harder." It HAS to.

The last year of Jesus was the terrifying, terrible year of His life and we follow in His footsteps. Is the servant above the Lord? "If he would follow Me," Jesus said, "he must take up his cross." What did the cross do to Jesus? It was the instrument upon which He died. What will my cross be? It will be the instrument upon which I die. But what a release! All heaven opened to Him, and so it will with us.

Adam, in the beginning, had a sensitivity to God; access to God; contact; he sensed God. That failure on Adam's part didn't finish God's walking. When Jesus came, He came to walk the earth again, that He might bring to man the Word of Life and Truth, and begin an intercourse of spiritual understanding. He walked the earth for what? Seeking; seeking; hungry for fellowship.

The thing that would please His heart most, I think, is to have your heart in sweet fellowship with Him, more than anything you ever do or think. Why? Because that is something that nobody in the world can live but YOU. He has millions of angels serving him; many serving here, but few loves. It is so much more beautiful to sit five minutes in His Presence, and love Him! May God walk and talk within us.

CHAPTER XVII

GRADUATION

It is our attitude toward Truth, and our power to receive that classifies us. Paul mentions three classes of people: natural; spiritual; carnal man. The thing which determines the class to which we belong, is our capacity to understand: our love of Truth; our embracing the Truth, and letting it work in us. We should ask ourselves the question: "Am I actually a lover of the Truth?"

Gradation is all through the New Testament. It speaks about children, even little children, and by and by about sons and grown-up sons. Do you see a development? That is God. There is nothing static in Him. Gradation is also mentioned with regard to food: milk, meat, and strong meat.

He sometimes gets the superfluous stuff, the non-essentials, out of the way. He says "Let us grow in grace and love." Two words in the Word of God have intrigued me: one is "TO GROW"; the other is "TO LEARN." There is nothing in the two words of instantaneous acquisition, or grasping or holding. Salvation may be in a moment, but growing, and learning are processes. I am glad to find that they even relate to our Lord in His human aspect. When he took up the human concept to manifest and show to God what the Adam should be, He was restricted to it, and He GREW in stature and knowledge. HE GREW; HE LEARNED!

"And though He were The Son of God, yet LEARNED He the things of God through a law of suffering." (Heb. 5:8) Well, that's the lovely Christ we have. Do you think we are exempt? No, Jesus said, "No scholar is above his master." We can grow just as much as we want to, and we can learn just as much as we want to. For both involve a process, but not an immediate possession. I can be saved in a moment, but it takes a lifetime to develop what God is after.

We are changed from one degree of glory to another. We are still being changed. Note how the Revelation Churches made a display of what they did.

"I know thy works (now don't bring out all that to Me), but I have somewhat to say to YOU."

God is here, and He has plenty of food, but our portion of it is determined by how we react to the Truth. Proverbs 30:8 says, "Feed me with food convenient for me." The original reads: "Feed me with food which is my daily portion." What food may feed one, may not feed another who may not be able to grasp that portion of the Word at all, because we are all living on different spiritual levels. Our powers of receptivity have to be built up, and the hunger has to be created in us so that God can meet us.

So many people say, "You have this, and you have that—God is good to this one, and God isn't good to that one." Now don't do that. When He gave, it says distinctly in Matthew 25:15: "He gave to each according to his ability." How many can see that giving was governed by the individual, and not by God. He gave according to their capacity. The giving was regulated by the instrument; not by God. Yet people always say, "God did this, and God did that, and gave that one such and such." That's not true. God gives according to the receptivity of the individual, the capacity that is them. Now, none of us is accountable for that; we wake up with what capacity we have.

In John 21, three kinds of sheep are mentioned: lambs (lambkins), sheep, sheep (old sheep), Jesus begins with the diminutive: "Pasture My little sheep." His first concern is His flock, but He is concerned with the potential sheep; not the old one. One can't do much with them.

That is why I covet young people, because their thought patterns haven't all been arranged for them; their little philosophies haven't all been cooked up by some evangelist or Bible teacher, or somebody else, and all fixed for them. I want young people who are freed, and cleared from a lot of that technique to which they have to surrender and die. I often say, "Don't read too much. You will probably have to die to all of it anyway."

John 21:15-17 says "So when they had dined, Jesus saith to Simon Peter, Simon, son of Jonas, lovest (agapao—love unto sacrifice) thou Me more than these? He saith unto Him, Yea Lord; Thou knowest that I love (phileo—am fond of) Thee. He saith unto him feed My lambs. He saith to him again the second time, Simon, son of Jonas, lovest (love unto sacrifice) thou Me? He saith unto Him, Yea Lord; Thou knowest that I love (am fond of) Thee. He saith unto him, Feed My sheep. He saith unto him the third time, Simon, son of Jonas, lovest (phileo—fond of) thou Me? Peter was grieved because He said unto him the third time, lovest thou Me? And he said unto Him, Lord, Thou knowest all things; Thou knowest that I love (am very fond of) Thee. Jesus saith unto him, Feed My sheep."

Peter can only come up to "phileo" —I am very fond of You; not "agapao"—a love unto sacrifice. Note: We get a beautiful lesson here. When we cannot measure up to the strong place He would have us reach, He comes down to us, and meets us in the measure of love of which we are capable. So the third time Jesus says, "Are you very fond of Me?" or "Am I dear to you?" This breaks poor Peter's heart, and he confesses, "Yea, Lord, Thou knowest all things; thou knowest that I am fond (phileo) of Thee (not agapao)."

There are different methods of feeding too, which are not brought out in translations. Notice that the original words are different:

1. Lambs—lambkins—graze. My lambkins; you (Peter-shepherds) have to go out and find the food; they are not safe to choose.

2. Sheep—immature—lesser sheep who yet have to be grazed; they are not yet safe or able to discern error.

3.   Sheep—old sheep—feed; should be able by now to be turned out into pasture, and have "their senses exercised to discern truth from error."

I ask the Lord to send me the people who will be helped. So I always pray to keep away the people who can't be helped, but bring in the people who need help, and know they need it, and are anxious to receive it. Then, I feel, that creates an atmosphere in which the Spirit of God can move. I have often prayed people out of the meeting, and prayed them in.

When Jesus taught, it was the same. He didn't have one message for everybody. He had a message for the multitude; peculiarly the message with physical phenomena, such as healings and visions; the things which would attract them physically. He used all of those as He taught in fascinating parables and stories, but, when He was alone with His disciples, Scripture says, "He expounded all things to them." Can you see the difference? "For without parables He did not speak to the multitude"; only with them. When He was alone with receptive hearts—some that He could coach a little more, He was able to open even more.

If we follow the gradation in the New Testament, illustrated by those who followed Him, we will be surprised to find He is always the center, and about Him moves this multitude; it gradually reduces and reduces, until it becomes quite a unique little group, who can really have an ear to hear. In Revelation it says over and over: "To him that hath an ear, let him hear"—those who have capacity to hear. So I pray, for those who have ears, to come.

CHAPTER XVIII

HEALING

Regarding healing: The miracle in the flesh will perish, but the miracle in the spirit—to make us into living spirits—will last through eternal ages. Do you want deliverance or development?

People get these strange ideas that God always fits into the same pattern. He did not raise every corpse that was being buffed!

God reaches the basic need by a physical distress.

I am always healed in spirit first, before it ever touches my body.

Christ's words are as much a miracle as His deeds. The very words He speaks are above the realm of nature and philosophy of man. The miracle of the

Word is always above the miracle of the deed—it lasts for ages, but the deed only for time. When He works a miracle on my spirit, it abides through the eternal ages. The miracle on my body is only for time, and the miracle dies with me.

We must learn this: God does not always do the things which He is able to do. He doesn't always want to do the things, because they are not always in His design and purpose. All things are possible, but all things are not always probable.

Now regarding the man who claimed all the promises for the healing of his mother of cancer, and, when it didn't work, came to me asking, "Why?" He never once said, "What are You doing, Lord?" He was telling the Lord what he wanted the Lord to do! If he had spent five minutes before the Lord praying and asking Him to speak to his heart, and had said, "Lord, You give me a Word concerning this situation; I don't know. You know all my natural human instincts and desires, but I don't know what Your purpose is in this thing at all, because You have that situation relating to a great scheme of which I have no knowledge at all. What is Your will concerning this?" Then He will reveal His will to you, and always give you some Word of promise which will carry you. He has done that many times. I have had to unlearn a lot I learned forty years ago; not because it was not scriptural, but the promise didn't pertain to that particular situation.

Second Peter 1:4 says the promises are given to us. The promises are given to us; we don't take them to Him. When the emergency comes, and the need comes, God, knowing us and the whole situation, will give us the Word. Now don't try to get it the first minute; it isn't like a Ouija board: one, two, three, bumble bee, I want a promise all for me. . . And then we get one and it doesn't work. Then we don't like it, so we put it back in the box, and then we pull out another one, and we say, "Oh, the Lord spoke to me!"

God has HIS WORD, and He has a Word for every occasion, and, if we will be honest with Him, whether we like the Word He gives us or not, that is not the point. If we go to find a Word we like which we think will bridge the chasm, and then it doesn't work; that is disastrous. He may give us a Word that we may really not relish very much, but when He gives it to us, we can take it, and go to God and say, "Oh Father, what is Your thought about this situation? Now, Father, I could find a lot of promises which I would like, but I don't know how to use them, because I don't know which one fits this. Now, speak to my heart."

It will take us a while to get still, and whatever Word He has, I don't care if it is the simplest thing, cherish that; hold it; that is fresh; a promise fresh from heaven, because God spoke it. We say, "Doesn't he speak through His Word?" Yes, but the Word in itself is a dead thing. If we go and find the promises, they are all dead. They have to be enlightened by the Spirit of God. When God speaks a Word it has two qualities about it. The Word which God speaks into our hearts has faith already with it, and it is creative. As soon as that Word gets into our hearts, it begins creating; bringing life; it has power. But a Word which we pick (now it is The Word of God; don't quarrel about that)—the one we pick has no life; no power. Let Him speak the Word; then we can go through with Him.

CHAPTER XIX

HOLY SPIRIT

After the fall and ruin, the Holy Spirit still moves as the life principle of God. He now groans throughout all creation, as well as in the heart of the believer, and waits for the day of triumph and consummation. He brooded over the earth in the beginning to bring it to its creation. Now He groans through us to bring it to its redemption.

The Holy Spirit will live in anybody who will let Him. We talk of the humiliation of Jesus in taking upon Himself the form of man. That's fine, but I think it's also tremendous to know that the Holy Spirit has never assumed a body of His own. He says, "I will dwell in you. You will be My temple."

Jesus says in John 16:13, "I have many things I would like to talk to you about; but you cannot now

take them, but afterward the Holy Spirit will lead
(guide) you into all Truth." It's a leading—that means
utter dependence.

These songs (see JWF's book of Hymns) came to
me in the Spirit. I remember standing with my guitar
singing songs in the Spirit I had never heard sung;
pouring out in the Spirit were the music and the song,
the whole thing born right out of that instrument,
more than once. Have you ever been in a meeting
where the Spirit would fall, and we would sing in the
Spirit that way? It was a real manifestation of the Holy
Spirit. But we don't have any of those early, lovely
manifestations any more—any Pentecost that I know
of. That was all very real. I am glad I came in in the
early days, because that lovely thing had not been
touched, nor tampered, nor meddled with by people,
and there was no one to spoil or channel it. You see,
it is in man's power to always channel it, label it, and
have it arranged. God doesn't like that.

Now the two characteristic marks of the early
Pentecost that I remember were originality in the
moving of the Spirit, and spontaneity. Those two
marks, I think are all blurred now. I have been in
Pentecostal meetings a lot, but even in this
outpouring that we

have now, those two marks are not evident. There was an originality of the Spirit, but no one today wants to find room for it. They encourage the Spirit and tell Him what to do! That is wrong! When the Holy Spirit wants to work, we don't need to encourage or instruct Him in a thing, but it has come to that method where He has no original design or pattern, because He is so coached by all the rest.

I always want to say, "Sit down; this is holy stuff; don't touch it." But you dare not do that. When the Holy Spirit had His way in those early days, He did unusual things which would be original and spontaneous—not studied, and no one planned for it. I have gone to meetings just dozens and dozens of times when not one would know who was going to have any part in the meeting at all. The Holy Spirit might use this person or another as a channel through whom he would provide the theme for that meeting. It would be the key for that gathering, and the meeting would center on that one theme.

Maybe the next night that person wouldn't have the Spirit on him at all, but another one would have a leading of the Spirit, and God would bring forth. It was spontaneous; it was not studied; we never had any programs made; in fact, we didn't know what they were. That can be maintained for a while—not too long. Religious flesh—not bad, vulgar, cussing, swearing, flesh, but religious flesh can spoil a thing as much as getting drunk. You don't have to get drunk to spoil it; just be religious. How many know you can be religious, and not spiritual.

I would like to see the spontaneity of the Spirit rather than the efforts of man encouraging and handling it. The things in God don't need that; they don't need that. They need flesh to be quiet in His Presence. I have been in meetings where we didn't have one moving at all —not a hymn—not a prayer—not a scripture lesson, and sat in the Presence of the Lord two hours without one single manifestation of any description; then get up and go home so refreshed one would think he had a spiritual bath! I don't see that any more.

What would our meetings today be like if anyone would dare to be quiet? It's like the two people who sat in a meeting; one sat so serenely, and so quietly, and then there was the extrovert: explosive, and demonstrative.

He was saying, "Glory! Hallelujah! Glory! Glory!" He said to the other man, "Haven't you any glory, brother?" The other man said, "Yes, mine is glory unspeakable!" I thought that was good. "Yes, mine is unspeakable, and full of glory." We don't need to arrange anything; just move with God. We can't regulate it. He would sometimes do the most surprising things, but we never knew how it would be. It can't last too long; man will always be there trying to manipulate the things of the Spirit.

Now concerning the word 'power' as used in the New Testament, we find our English translators have combined two Greek words into one. There needs to be a distinction made here:

1.   Dunamis: The power to execute— always His. (Acts 1:8; Luke 1:35)

2.   Exousia: Authority: that is always mine. (John 10:18) You will notice that He says, "When He, (the Holy Ghost) is come upon you, then things will happen." Why? Because the ability, the power to execute, the power to make good, the power to bring the thing through (dunamis) that is always His. He only lends the power to us, when the occasion demands; the dunamis; to make that thing do. Then the Holy Spirit comes upon us, the ability is ours, and then He lifts it. Why? To keep us dependent and humble, where we belong.

Now the other meaning of the word 'power' is seen where Jesus said, "I have power to lay down my life, and I have power to take it up again: The word 'power' (exousia) in this verse means authority. He went into the grave, and He did not come forth of His own power! He had authority, but God had to exercise the power (dunamis)! God, through the eternal Spirit raised Him from the dead.

The power of authority, and the power to execute, are two different things.

Every little while, as occasion demands, He drops the Holy Spirit—the dunamis—over me, and I have the ability to do that which His will calls for. Immediately after, I couldn't do that thing to save my life.

We receive power to do the thing which He permits. He will give us only enough power as the occasion demands, and after that, we might as well sit down. God retains the right to dispense the power. God is yet sovereign. He only gives the measure when the occasion arises. That is why none of us can take the initiative to do things.

The naked Word hasn't any power at all, but when He speaks that Word to my heart, the Spirit quickens it, and it becomes creative. Faith and power come with the creative Word.

What is the attitude I am to take? Lord, speak to my heart the things for which You want me to believe.

Indicate to me what You want me to do in this situation. Then when He speaks the Word to my heart it is like dynamite—that thing will hold me through anything, and the devil can't hold anything against me when God gives me the Word.

"And there was delivered unto Him the book of the prophet Isaiah. And when He had opened the book, He found the place where it was written . . ." (Luke 4:17) He had definite instruction: it was Holy Ghost dictation. It does not say He hunted through the Scriptures until He found a passage which He always enjoyed. So many times the reading is what we like; not what He directs us to read. Oh, that He could only direct—direct in the choice of a hymn; a testimony; a verse, or what He desires! So many times the whole force and power of a meeting may hinge on a hymn suggested by the Holy Spirit.

Everything in Spirit moves in rhythm. Rhythm is all the way through Scripture—ascending and descending, moving in a rhythmic movement. We may be sharing, ministering, teaching, but not for long; we have to come back. This is His divine process:

Ascent = Glory, revelation, illumination, visitation.

Descent = Execution, demonstration.

Ascent = Jesus went up to Jerusalem —revelation.

Descent = He went down to Nazareth —"and was subject unto them."

Ascent = He went up the Mt. of Transfiguration— glory, revelation.

Descent = He went down to the foot of the mountain to the demoniac (you and I)—execution and demonstration.

Ascent = He went up to Calvary.

Descent = He went down to the tomb.

Ascent = He arose and ascended.

Descent = He has to come back again; it isn't finished.

CHAPTER XX

JESUS

We forget we have a victorious Head; He is crowned, and all power is vested in Him in heaven and in earth. We are only cells in the Body. We don't have to worry; just look at the birds, etc.

He is the center of everything; He is the center of the universe, and everything should verge to Him. Our hearts should all the time move toward Him.

If we know HIM; we know enough.

The glory is not a divine attribute; it is a divine effulgence. Jesus could leave that glory to redeem man. "He took upon Himself the form of a servant."; the "morphe"; all the essential elements of man. (Phil. 2:7)

The divine Son of God is the core of His being. That can't be tempted, but this human which He has wrapped around Him can be tempted. How many know there is a "tree" in the wilderness? From God's side, the testing is to harden everything in Him like steel. From the enemy's side, it is unto destruction. As Man, he says, "I can of Myself do nothing— not My will . . ."

Jesus' vocation was to do the will of God. The Holy Spirit is the power by which the will of God is executed—the dynamic.

I want to talk about Jesus in one of the characters He bears. He has many names, and He represents many characters. He is One in Himself, but He has many phases of life and character. While He was here on the earth, He called Himself the SON of MAN many times. I made a study of it, and it has given me new perspective in my vision of Him. He is projected out there, and I see Him in greater light than when I am too close. Sometimes, some things need to be looked at, and examined very closely; other times we lose all perspective when we get too close. We have to get away from them. For instance, we can be right in the mountains, and not see them, but if we are at a distance, when the light is just so, we get a different effect of the mountains. The impact upon our sense of beauty is one that we don't get while we are living right in them, because we need perspective.

We need it in our thinking; we need it in our approach to God; we need it in our study. People become involved in their own individual problems, and their own interests—that's good—, but too much of that is self-centered.

When I was caught in that jam, God pulled me out of it. He told me, "You have to have perspective. Don't stay so close. When you are closest to the situation, you lose your sense of value, because there is nothing with which to contrast it. That's very fatal; your perspective is wrong. Now, come on, leave your situation where you are right there; now come on. I won't hurt you; don't be scared. Now come along with Me over here."

It's rather daring to get out of yourself for a minute. We are so self-centered. When he begins to dislodge us, and we stand over there, He'll say, "Now, do you see how it is?" When we are too localized, we lose our sense of value. That's one little fault we have as Christians, who love Him, walk with Him, serve Him. It took the Lord a long time to thrash that thing through with me.

We have to find out who we are, and a little bit about ourselves, because we are too self-centered. He wants us to trust Him with the most sacred items in our hearts, but if we are fearful, He can't help us. We have to be daring enough to say: "Here is this situation, Lord," and then let Him work.

Being identified with us, He calls Himself: Son of Man. He was the perfect ideal concept of man. What did God make when He made a man? He was not only Savior, but He was God's ideal of a man. How do we know this? Because He calls Himself the Last Adam.

He calls Himself Son of Man 85 times in the gospels: 32 times in Matthew, 15 times in Mark, 26 times in Luke and 12 times in John.

The Holy Son of God could mask Himself. He was sinless, but dependent, just as much as Adam was dependent. No sin ever touched Him, but He assumed a role of deep humility, and said, "I will become that kind of man—dependent." For example, when He worked His miracles, He said of Himself, "I do not do these by Myself; what I see the Father do, that I do." Why does He say this? Because He is playing the part of that Adam, and the glorious aspect of the whole manifestation is Godward. He will redeem man, but His first thought is focused Godward.

"I will live unto the glory of God. I will become an obedient servant unto God, and in this plan will be the redemption of mankind. My first thought is Godward; that He might have the satisfaction He never found in Adam." God found it in the Last Adam. He identified Himself as man at the baptism. He prayed because He had to pray.

On the Mt. of Transfiguration, the glory broke out from WITHIN. It was concealed all the while He was walking this earth. The Word is careful to say that the glory came from within; not that something came upon Him. Nobody knew the Miracle Who walked this earth. But you see, when Jesus comes to maturity, it is released, and He is glorified. His garments—His body were like a tremendous, shining light; transfigured. We shall yet reach such a state by a glorified body. Adam never should have seen death. He should have seen glorification. No idea of death was in God's thought for Adam. The Last Adam moved to the place of glorification.

What isolation! I think that Jesus must have been the loneliest of men because He had no one with whom to share His exaltation when He stood upon the mountain top; no one to understand His cryptic words, nor to decipher His writing in the sand. He chose an inner circle, but their vision was so dim that even by His side they were a world away from Him! I think, perhaps, when coming down from some transcendent place, the flame of mystic revelation was upon His face.

In the temptation in the wilderness, Jesus was with wild beasts, but none of them touched Him. He had dominion over them. He could speak to the fish, and they came up with a coin. He could speak to the storm that the devil was raging, and there was calm. The enemy is the prince of the air, you know: the prince of all those elements, and sometimes he likes to bring on a ferocious, terrific time. It isn't God at all; it's the devil. The devil was always out to kill Him. When He was a little baby, the devil tried to kill Him, and later, in Nazareth, he tried to throw Him over a precipice. He always wanted to get Him out of the way, but God wouldn't let him. Jesus had authority over the elements: "Be quiet!" That was authority; the authority of a perfected man talking!

Jesus took the human nature in which He voluntarily chose to move. He took that nature up, and wrapped it about Him, but inside He was eternally the Son of God; the Eternal Son of God; one of the Trinity; but He chose to limit Himself. He laid aside so much; not His deity; not His divinity. He still maintained that divinity, but He said, "I will throw about Me this human nature with its limitation, and with its utter dependence. I have to be the Last Adam. There was a first one. I have to be, before God, the Last Adam."

What else did He have to be? The perfect man that God wanted Adam to become. He was demonstrating what that perfect human being should have done. I wish you would make a distinction, when you read of Jesus walking and moving—can you distinguish between a supernatural manifestation of God, and also a manifestation of a miracle that comes from Jesus? He moved many times as man, when people thought it was only God. No. It was the forces and powers of an ideal, perfected, human concept of life, without sin, limited and dependent, which could do things.

God said to Adam: "Now I have given you, potentially, powers for that in your human construction. If you will abide and live with Me in My will and purpose, these powers will all function in your life. Keep yourself exposed to Me; and I can cause these things to move naturally; not as additional powers added to you as a human being."

That is the marvelous expression of what God wanted the first Adam to do, which he failed to do through sin and disobedience. But the restored; the real Adam; moving in God; in His will; could have this marvelous expression. He could have dominion over all the earth. He could say, "Fish, come," and they would come. As the Second Adam, Jesus is a striking, wonderful example of what the first Adam could have been.

I want you to see His utter dependence in His manifestation as the Last Adam. Jesus doesn't act independently in anything. He is the most dependent creature. He restricts His fashion of living to the fact that He is the Last Adam.

In creation, God made man limited and dependent; two chief characteristics of the human. Man is dependent upon God, for there is no life in himself; he is a created being, and he is limited to moving within the sphere of the natural bounds. Of the human nature, God said, "I will make it dependent and limited. I will make him dependent so that man cannot of himself do anything, but, as I give him life and strength, and My will is revealed, he will take his will and attach it to Mine, and We will work together."

Man didn't originate anything. God originated all the planning; Adam was to execute it as limited and dependent man.

Jesus was a completely consecrated instrument in the hands of God for the display of God's grace and power. "He that hath seen Me hath seen the Father. I don't originate anything. The Words that I speak (the message), are God's; the power that I have is God's. I am the Last Adam. I am functioning, but there is no independence in Me; nor in any of the Trinity."

Concerning the Spirit, He says, "When He, the Spirit, is come, He will take of the things that I have given, and show them unto you." He will not speak from Himself—not: "He will not speak of Himself." ('Of' is a poor preposition.) He speaks of Himself in His ministry hundreds of times, but He never speaks from Himself as an authority. "He will take the things that I have given, and speak them unto you." Why? To keep that strange dramatic unity in the whole scheme: the Father, the Son, the Holy Spirit:

The Trinity in His teaching;

The Trinity in His message;

The Trinity in His method of work.

So He says, "If you have seen Me, you have seen the Father, for We are One. What I do, that's the Father working through Me; for I preach what the

Lord God Jehovah gives Me; I am an instrument in His hands."

I like His yieldedness and His absolute surrender. It astounds me! The more I see Him, the more I marvel at this Christ; the most tremendous character that ever walked the earth; the most sublime personality that ever touched the earth! (John 14:8-11)

The last thing Jesus ever offered back to God was His spirit. Jesus' life was one of: Obedience, devotion; utter dependence.

He had to do a lot of things before He could teach. Acts 1:1 "The former treatise have I made, O Theophilus, of all that Jesus began both to do and teach."

In Jesus' teaching, He never did too much with effect. He dealt with causation. In the Old Testament, God always dealt with the immediate: the act; that's as far as it could go. Adultery— kill! Don't you think Jesus was cognizant of wrong? Certainly. Did He pick at the wrong? He went back to causation, and helped the poor creature with the thing that caused it. Causation is our field of motivation.

The Old Law said, "That is wrong!" The New Testament says, "That is wrong; what made it wrong?" Listen to Jesus' teaching:

"It has been said an eye for an eye, a tooth for a tooth . . . but I say unto you . . ., something has provoked that deed, let's see if we can't get that thing fixed. It has been said, thou shalt not commit adultery, but let's go back to what caused the adultery. He that hateth his brother has already committed murder . . ." You say you can't prove it; where is the knife and the pistol? That kind of murder isn't done with knives and pistols. Don't you know many people have been slain, because of a hateful spirit on the part of some person? The root of the thing is our field of motivation.

Christianity is not a philosophy. It is a way of life. We may make philosophic patterns for its detailed movings— that's legitimate—but we cannot reduce it to any philosophic form with which we are familiar. We are treating it from one level when it is resting in another. It was never intended to be pulled down to fit into our modern thinking and ways.

Jesus didn't come to bring a new philosophy by which we could live; He came to bring us life: a redemption to bring us out of the chaos of an old setup in every form, through a marvelous redeeming action. That redeeming action moves into every field of our lives and beings. It isn't a philosophy; it is life. "I have come to bring you life." He didn't say, "I have come to redeem you from hell." He has, hasn't He? Yes, but He never allowed His teaching to move between these two points to which it has been reduced today. Our popular evangelism, and most of the popular teaching about Christ, move between these two: heaven and hell. Escape hell, and go to heaven. Jesus never taught that way. We never can find a message that he preached on heaven, or on hell. If those are the two great paramount issues, then why didn't the Son of God ever preach about them?

What are the two pivotal points, then? They are life and death. So we come quite amiss; we come quite short of what He intended us to have. "I have come to bring you life." If we have that life, we escape hell. Don't make issues of things He never made issues of at all.

CHAPTER XXI

KINGDOM OF GOD

In Luke 17:20-21, where He speaks of "the kingdom of God"—this kingdom realm that we live in—Jesus didn't call it "the kingdom." He called it "the realm" and I like it much better; Many of our translators are using the word "realm" now, and they should, because our word "kingdom" has these connotations of bugles, banners, horses, chariots, and thrones. He isn't talking about that. He is talking about a vast realm of spiritual reality. All spiritual reality is in this one realm called the kingdom of the Spirit, which is the new realm into which we are birthed. We have to live in this realm, just the same as in the world into which we are born. We have to learn to adjust ourselves to it.

When He introduces us into this kingdom, He introduces us to a vast realm. In that realm He has angels, paradise, and all that world; a domain; a kingdom over which God rules; over which there is jurisdiction and purpose. In creation, God said man should reign or rule over a great domain. In that kingdom are various kingdoms—mineral, animal, vegetable.

When He made a man, He made a vast new realm consisting of the human concept of life. He made us human beings with capacities and potentials that we don't know anything about. God was to be glorified in this vast field or realm. The realm remained after man became a sinner, but there was no King; no authority that the realm was designed for. That kingdom, without a King, waited for a King. This realm is in every heart, waiting for the King to come in to possess it. Jesus said to the Pharisees, "The kingdom of God is resting within you." He seeks to possess that kingdom, and He longs to get power over it. It is waiting for Him to possess.

Scofield calls the kingdom, "salvation" which is wrong. God brings a spiritual thing in. He is enthroned in our hearts. We enter this spiritual kingdom through a new birth. He is reclaiming that kingdom every time He comes into a heart. "He came to seek and save that which was lost." His redemption not only includes man, but all creation. This whole universe, because of sin, has to be redeemed. On the cross, the blood touched the earth first; "Cursed be the ground." That is the first thing that was brought under judgment.

"Unless you are born of the Spirit, you cannot see (understand) the kingdom of God." (John 3:3)

"And from the days of John the Baptist until now the kingdom of heaven suffereth violence and the violent take it by force." (Matthew 11:12) "Taking the kingdom of heaven by violence" means stress, and suffering on our part in order to possess this realm into which He has birthed us. We have great joy and all that, but that is sort of a sideline. To me, the life of the Spirit is, in a sense, the most tragic thing I can get into. It's the opposite of what I think it is. It takes all my struggle, power, and strength to possess it.

When God told the Children of Israel to go into Canaan, He said, "I have given it to you." In a little while He said also, "Go in to possess it." This was a potential term. They were not qualified yet to possess it. The land was full of giants, and walled cities, which required a struggle for its possession.

I never have known more about the power of the devil than when I got the baptism. It was then that I found I couldn't take possession in there (Canaan) without a terrific struggle. "Whatsoever your foot (faith) possesses," that is yours. Possessing your land is Truth, which becomes personalized. "He will not suffer thy foot to be moved." (Psa. 121:3) We have to get into the realm of God through many a trouble. The Children of Israel got into the land by a gift, but they didn't get possession of that land except by force. It is grasped by force.

". . . We must through much tribulation enter into the kingdom of God." (Acts 14:22b) Through great distress, trouble, and suffering, we enter the kingdom, this realm of spiritual reality and living. That kingdom is entered through much tribulation, trouble and discipline. Why? Because that is necessary to release you and me from the bondages which would hinder and wreck the lovely design and objective that God has for your life and for mine. God's objective for man is to glorify Him and to give Him pleasure. How will one person glorify God? By bearing a cross which is almost impossible to share. How will another? By bearing that suffering with Him, which nobody knows but that one and the Lord. In the end he will see he has glorified God.

"Though He slay me," yet God's grace is holding me; the Holy Spirit is holding me. "Though He slay me," yet will I hold on to Him, and move with Him. Life, if you want to know, is the most tragic thing; at least I found it so. You can love the will of God, but you can't always enjoy everything that is in the will of God. No, it says, "Jesus ENDURED" things. He endured how? "For the joy that was set before Him." He endured this life, the cross, and all for what? "For the JOY that was set BEFORE Him;" not the joy which He experienced.

CHAPTER XXII

LIFE

Accept life—God knows all about it. Turn your life over to Him. Let Him show you how to work it out.

If you learn to interpret life, you can accept it.

Regarding high, ecstatic points in life, we can't maintain the emotional stimuli of that high point. We couldn't live under it. We are not made to; our spirits are made to go up, and become acquainted with the realm of spiritual reality, and then come down again, and live it out in practical life.

Talents were given to each servant; not sinner, in Matthew 25:14-30. Talents here means the responsibility of life which He deposits in us. God is never partial. What have you done with the gift of your life? It can be wonderfully invested and multiplied—the life, light, truth, illumination; whatever He has deposited in you. I am only responsible for what I am. The capacity is varied in each. How many would like to have the burden and responsibility of the five talent man?

The reward has nothing to do with a material thing; it was a spiritual thing. Someday He will hold me accountable for my use or abuse of it, i.e. life (talent). Will you invest it in a thing that will bring a return, and result to the glory of God? Or will you squander it so that it won't have a return? The responsibility of life and vision—what avenue will you use?

I say to young people, "Make a good choice here which will carry you through the ages. We can't come back again and make it." What decision we make, guarantees, and puts a qualifying character mark on us, which is projected into the next age: He said it in the New Testament regarding faithfulness. "He that is faithful over a little—I will elevate that quality of faithfulness which I have worked in you—not the things you have been doing. All this work you did was the technique. I was not interested in that. That was the medium which I used: all that you did worked in you. I am bringing to pass in you a quality of faithfulness. It has taken your lifetime to accomplish in you what I was after, and that is what I will multiply tenfold in the next age.—I will make you ruler over ten cities."

Now that doesn't mean He is going to make you ruler in Timbuctoo over ten cities. I don't want you to think that. He is talking about spiritual things using the symbol of ten cities. Don't get hung up on that. No, He is looking for these qualities—they are abstract, but real.

So He says, "I've found in you a quality called faithfulness, and you were faithful over the least thing; that's the thing I want projected, and multiplied tenfold."

Won't it be wonderful to feel that all this living wasn't in vain after all! We had to have all the discipline to produce the quality of faithfulness. Then we say, "Look, Lord, what I did!" No. He said, "I'm not concerned with that." Did you notice in that story of those talents, when they came to deliver their response, and stand before Him, Jesus never said a thing about any of the works they did? I said, "Lord! You didn't even thank them."

Do you know what the Lord said? He told me, "Whatever was worthwhile, I had to do it, because it was Spirit-wrought." He doesn't thank Himself for anything He does!

How many can see the emphasis in our Christian world is completely out of order today? The emphasis is on: "To the work! To the work!" I say, "What are you building a church for unless the Lord is in it? If the Lord tells you to build a church, build it. If He doesn't tell you any such thing, then be still."

He is looking at us; He is training us; disciplining us. God says, "I'm giving you these little things to teach you. I want them to work faithfulness, love, and charity in you through this medium. I let you go as a missionary. Now you thought you were going to bring all the world to the feet of the Lord."

We aren't big enough to do that; we are too little. God is big enough, though. He may not call some other man to the mission field at all, but let him serve where he is. This same man may cry, and say, "That other man is over there saving the heathen, and I can't be over there." God says, "Don't worry," but we get worried about it, because we don't see God working in our everyday pattern of life. We don't seem to know much about Him. He only puts these activities into our pattern for their reflex action; not to encourage God, but as we react to these activities, we are changed. We are not the same creatures. God didn't even thank them for their works. No work is acceptable to Him except that which is wrought in the Spirit, and no work is acceptable to Him except that which has gone through death.

So, for what has a man to be thanked? The very first word Jesus says to all those churches in Revelation is, "I know thy works. Now sit down. I have something to say to YOU. Don't come here with your arms filled with all the things you did. That's nice; it kept you busy; kept you out of jail, and some other things. Well done. Good and faithful servant." The emphasis is on the SERVANT and not the works: What is the work accomplishing in this man while he is engaged in these activities? It produces three qualities:

1. "WELL DONE"— It has to be correctly motivated, and wrought in the power of the Spirit.

2. "GOOD"— In Swedish or Norwegian the word for good, is "God-like". It comes from the same root word. The very thing that has occupied you has wrought in you a God-like quality, which is reflected in your character.

3. "FAITHFUL"— You can be faithful when you can't be successful. It isn't that you are so successful, but you are faithful. On the basis of this faithfulness, you

have the quality that He wants to expand in the next age. (Matt. 25:14-30)

If you are selling peanuts, sell them to the glory of God. If you are a carpenter, be a carpenter to the glory of God. If you are washing dishes, wash the dishes to the glory of God. Why? It isn't just washing the dishes—it's the spirit back of it. There are some people never called to go to the mission field, or to preach.

In Luke 15, we read of an awful famine in a far country. The word 'prodigal' is not in the Bible, but "younger son" is. The phrase "riotous living", used in this story, means extravagant expenditure of living. The life was misspent, or didn't bring the return or meet the objective for which it was meant. It was squandered; it had no return; it was wasted. God received no return from His investment in the life of the younger son. Your life can be lost in its most cultured form, because it never yet functioned in the field where it was meant to be. Life had lost its aim, and never found it.

No man fed him, because it is not in his nature to feed a spiritual desire; nothing in the world can feed that! We never find any satisfaction, or meaning to life until we come back to our first primary principle, and we enter into the thought that: "The heart was made for God; neither can it rest until it rests in

God." (St. Augustine) The younger son never came to himself—that evasive ego; he never came to that until . . . (Luke 15:11, 32)

If life doesn't obtain the objective for which it is intended, it is "riotous living". "Riotous living" doesn't bring back the income—the purpose for which it was intended. It's the wrong investment. Life has lost its objective and purpose in unfortunate, wasted living. But God is interested in its restoration; not its punishment.

In John 4:5-42, we have the story of the woman at the well. She had had five husbands, and the one she was living with was not her husband. Five is suggestive; it is an incompletion; an exhaustion. It is always a five—five avenues in which the hungry heart moves out on—five senses too. We have the avenue of five senses to move out on before we strike reality in God.

We can almost name them:
1.   Intellectual research

2.   Love

3.   Service

4 & 5.   Any kind of aimless pursuits toward which we push and focus our lives.

She had had five husbands, but never found what her heart wanted. We have all these husbands to which our hearts are united, but there is no marriage; no union; no completion, because the heart was never made for it. But when she says, "Come, behold a MAN!–I have found THE MAN. Behold, here is the Answer to my life problem! My life has been pushing out through all these avenues." These five men represent various things in an individual life. Think of the pursuits we have made before we find THE MAN!–THE Answer!–The ONE! Come behold HIM!–He is the Center. I feel any testimony or any life which is organized and centered about anything but the Presence, and the Personality of that dynamic Christ is mis-centered.

Everything that God brings, and permits to come into our lives, has an objective; it has a reason. We have to learn to interpret it.

We will never grow without a conflict and battle. Where there is life; there is opposition. Note the flowers, as they push through the hard soil.

CHAPTER XXIII

LOVE OF GOD

The first vocation of personality is expression; it is basic. Man is to love; to live; to get out; he is made with potential powers. Out in the world, man has never found the proper avenue through which he can express himself, to really live.—No Christ—no essential element of Life. He came to bring Life.

Oh, the persistency of the love of God in seeking; the social instinct of God! We see it in the Trinity—God the Father, God the Son, and God the Holy Spirit. There is an interchanging, reciprocating, oneness relationship among Them. We see the social God in creation; He is always after us. He is interested; He persists. Note the first question in the Bible: "Adam, where art thou?" He is still asking our lost, broken down, alienated Adam, "Oh, heart, where are you? Oh, soul, where are you?" Oh, the persistency of the love of God! In Genesis He is a seeking God, and in Revelation He is still pursuing, seeking: "Behold, I stand at the door and knock . . ." Oh, the persistency of the heart of God in seeking! God is not defeated, even though man may fail. He comes and visits Abraham—still comes to him. He comes to Moses; the longing, loving heart of God.

Then He comes to the Tabernacle. The purpose of the Tabernacle in the wilderness was, as God said, "Let them make Me a Sanctuary that I may dwell among them." (Ex. 25:8) God gets a little bit nearer; He tries to get just as near to broken humanity as He can. He desires to bring us back to our original purpose, and glorious destiny. We were made for the purpose of glorifying Him, and having communion and fellowship with Him. By and by, there is a temple—a place where God manifests Himself.

Then comes Jesus; the Son from the Father's bosom—God manifesting Himself in the flesh. "The Word became flesh and tabernacled among us." (John 1:14) He walks again with man on earth, and comes oh, so near! Again we see the persistency of the love of God.

God, in the power of the Spirit, will come even closer to the heart, and live in the very body of the individual who will let Him. The sweet Spirit of God; the breath of God; the Third Member of the Trinity, has only your body and mine. I had to apologize to Him for it.

Have you ever apologized to Him? Jesus had a body given Him: "A body Thou hast prepared for Me." But the Holy Spirit has none but ours to live in.

Now it is the Body, the Church; that becomes the spiritual house of God, built of living stones. (Eph. 2:22; 1 Pet. 2:5) It is the individual heart that is the present dwelling place of God on earth. "He dwelleth not in temples made with hands."

Oh, the persistency of the love of God to come, and touch a life; to get hold of a man! The love of God comes to this poor, distorted, human being, and says, "I can save; cleanse; fill you, bring you back to coordination, and live in you, if you will let Me." Think of Him living in our bodies today! Some day the Holy Spirit will have our glorified bodies to live in!

CHAPTER XXIV

MAN

Man was made for God's pleasure and glory. God is seeking the glory which is due His name. He is seeking the pleasure which His loving heart has long sought in humanity. So, He always came in the cool of the evening, and He said to Adam, "Possess the earth; I have given you all the potentials for it. I have blessed you; given you all the intelligence that is necessary; cooperate with me, and possess this world. Bring it into subjection; release all its secrets of nature. Release all of these glorious, hidden things that are mysterious and strange." All that glorious, marvelous concept of life was hidden away in the heart of God, and He wanted it to come forth in man.

"Do My will, and it shall flow. Let your will be united with Mine; It will be one.

I will show you.

I will reveal to you.

I will show you the secrets, and you, in obedience to Me, free from the hampering, and all the bondages of this horrible sin that's in the world, freed from it, thou shalt move out in a glorious, glorious pattern."

God wanted this in His original thought and purpose. He says, "Adam, choose with Me; don't argue."

But, you see, the enemy, long, long before creation here, missed the whole thing in heaven. Fallen, now this enemy who had been cast out of the heavens, with a third of the angels with him, in the enemy's resistance to God, and in his defiance, says, "Will you have a creation? I'll damn it!" That's the eternal, everlasting purpose of Satan; to defeat the things of God; to blast; to ruin; to steal; to kill; to destroy.

But we have a Redeemer; Oh, glorious Christ! Eternal Redeemer! You have paved the way back. You have defeated him. He is a defeated foe. He is defeated. You told us a little about the redemption. Help us to receive it in all simplicity.

The highest vocation of any spiritual manifestation is worship and adoration; not service. You can't define man; you describe him.

The tree of life causes us to know that in us dwelleth no life. God made man dependent and limited.

The tree of knowledge of good and evil is for our development; to release all the potentials that are hidden in us.

"Adam, I have blessed you, and am pleased with the product of your creation. Now I want to be pleased with a performance of it. That will come by a law of testing and proving." Probationary law governs all growth. "And the Lord God commanded the man, saying, of every tree of the garden thou mayest freely eat: but of the tree of the knowledge of good and evil thou shalt not eat of it; for in the day that thou eatest thereof thou shalt surely die." (Gen. 2:16, 17) Just in the command there is a temptation, a testing. The subjects here, Adam and Eve, should not consider whether it is a good command or not; the command comes from an all-wise God. God cannot do anything that is not fair. He can do no injustice. He cannot lie; steal, or do evil. He is all holy love in His essence. His foreknowledge does not compel Adam to sin. In his foreknowledge, He already had a Lamb slain.

His foreknowledge doesn't destroy my individuality or personality, but the rest of my days He works, transforming, remaking, converting, recasting, until I can become partaker of the image and likeness of the Son of God.

It is so secure to be in a place of dependence.

Man is not to live by bread alone, but because he is a spiritual being, he, first of all, has to have contact in the spirit with God. Man is, first of all, spirit, and should live under the power and inspiration of the Spirit.

Spirit—soul—body. Man always says: body—soul—spirit. Why? Because man is body conscious first, and knows little about this spirit, but knows a lot about the body. God always says: "Spirit, soul, and body" because His concern is primarily with the spirit. He is not too concerned about the body. It's only the house that we live in; the vehicle.

The body, the flesh, is a sacred, holy instrument, and the redemption of God covers every aspect of our being. There is a trinity of being: spirit—soul—body.

There is a trinity of personality: intellect—emotions—will.

There are two characteristic marks which govern in our human nature capacity, and in the structural law of being:

1.   We are limited.

2.   We are utterly dependent upon God. We have no independence outside of Him. He never gives His power (in the Greek —"exousia" and "dunamis") to anyone. He lent His power to Adam.

We are not on a picnic; we are in a warfare. We are engaged in a battle. We are in a tremendous process of being extricated, and conformed. God is dealing with us drastically; sometimes most ferociously, and sometimes very tenderly. He wants to extricate us; to get us on the ground where we belong, with our vision where it should be, and to teach us how to walk with Him in the Spirit.

The discipline I may call forth from God takes a lifetime. It is good we don't see very much before; He can't trust us with it. If I had known what I would have to go through the last twenty-five years, I don't know if I would have had the courage to face it.

Adam was perfect in his potential: untouched by sin when he stood there at creation, but he was not perfectly developed. "Adam, I don't expect you to know it all, but I will reveal to you the secrets, and you can possess this whole place down here. I'll keep revealing to you the secrets; the knowledge; the whys; the hows; and as you abide in Me; come to Me; and deal with Me, and I deal with you, you will grow and develop."

Never get your nature, and character confused. Adam had a perfect, God-given nature, but the character he built himself. How? By all the ten thousand choices he made.

We are too tied up with this ego-centric thing that we have been living with here. If we could just step over there, and judge it with the Lord, that would be a little sign of maturity. ". . . Lord, will You hold me while You look at it?" We have to be held, because sometimes we are quite faint when we know what this ego is like. Then we can side with Him against that ego. We choose to side against it; our choice is with Him. When we are in agreement with His choice, we are perfectly safe, but our own choice is not safe.

I am not what I am in my intellect, or in my emotions, but I am what I am in my WILL!

CHAPTER XXV

MUSIC

I don't always enjoy hymns and music used in some places. Some songs annoy me. They have a rhythm, and a tempo that is not in rhythm, and in gear with what I feel in my spirit, and it annoys me.

We have so few hymns going back to God. Most of them are salvation hymns. There are three kinds of hymns:

1.   Experience hymns center on self.

2.   Prayer hymns are for something or someone.

3.   Worship hymns are directed to Him.

He knows our limitations, but when the Spirit keeps moving, He makes one lovely song—our songs, our singing seems very shallow as against the melodies, and the glory, and worship in heaven. Of course, it's very broken, and seems very shallow, but it's the best that we have. "Dear Lord, look on our hearts, and read them; receive from us what little we have."

CHAPTER XXVI

NEW BIRTH

In this dispensation, the Holy Spirit brings us into a relationship with God as sons. We have a heavenly Father. In the Old Testament, He is never revealed as a Father, and we as His little children. When Jesus comes, He makes a new relationship with the Father, and now we are to be born of the Spirit into a new family relationship. Israel never was born of the Spirit. The new man is birthed on Calvary.

The new birth is birthing us into a new conscious contact with divine reality. It releases us from that old Adamic setup. We are launched into orbit; space; and how big is space? Don't try to answer! The Holy Spirit, Who brought this marvelous Truth, is the only One who can reveal it, and interpret it. With all the background I have had, I have to sit down, and become a child, and say, "Lord, You have to tell me . . ." I find in the Word a continuity, a way, or thought, or a scheme. He is a wonderful God, but a heavenly Father. Jesus is a great Redeemer, but He says, "I am your Brother."

When it comes to salvation, we have to start with the knowledge of the Truth; then faith reaches out its hands, and takes that Truth from its mental processes, and "with the HEART man believeth".

CHAPTER XXVII

NEW CREATION

We go home under the overshadowing of His wings, and when the pressures come, remember that the overshadowing is where He works His miracle. It is not in the open. How shall these things be of bringing forth the Christ Child? How shall these things be that a new creation be birthed in us unto its fullness? It will be birthed under the shadow of the Almighty. Shadows are rather dark, but if Jesus puts us in the shadows, say, "Lord, work a miracle".

"In the beginning God." Now we don't know how many million years have gone by between that and the next verse in Genesis. We don't know. "In the beginning He created the heavens and the earth," but it "BECAME" a chaotic wreck through some cataclysm. "And the earth was (became) without form and void." (Gen. 1:2) We don't know what judgment ever came upon the earth to bring it to the chaos that God started with.

God doesn't start, and make crazy things. They become crazy, ugly, and disturbed through sin. He never makes a thing imperfect. What He does is perfect. He made, in the beginning, a perfect world; marvelous; beautiful; and some cataclysm, which He is not pleased to tell us, took place. I never snoop to find out; I keep my nose out of business that He doesn't want to talk to me about. I don't tease God. If God wants me to know some things, He will tell me.

The earth BECAME that chaotic mass; that great chasm; that terrifying chasm and darkness, through some judgment of God. Millions of ages passed, and there was an upheaval between the two forces of right and wrong; good and bad.

The sea is always the consuming, rasping, restless thing that would consume, but the earth becomes victorious. God blesses the EARTH. He brings the EARTH out of that chaotic mass. When He brings forth creation, the Word says the "Holy Spirit moved upon the deep". The Holy Spirit "BROODED" (in Hebrew) over the deep. It is the same word that carries the thought of incubation, and brings life. This brooding is like to a hen setting on her eggs. The Holy Spirit "BROODED" over the deep, and God's creative Word brought forth the glorious creation that we have through the power of the Spirit. This Holy Spirit has been brooding over this universe long before we had the world. The eternal urge of the Spirit, the consuming urge of the Spirit, is the pulse of God.

Even though God saves us, how many know He doesn't throw away the old nature. That's left intact, because He said, "Likewise reckon ye also yourselves to be dead indeed unto sin, but alive unto God through Jesus Christ our Lord." The fact that I am to reckon myself out of that old creation is evidence that it is still there. We don't have to live under its power. We have one personality, but we have two fields for its demonstration: (1) an old creation in which we can move if we want to; and (2) a brand new creation, and a new nature in which we may move. The old creation is still intact, but we have the victory of the Holy Spirit to keep identifying ourselves as a new creature in Christ Jesus, independent of the old creation; it's still there, however.

As to my new creation, He says, "Walk in newness of life; reckon; count yourself dead unto the old nature, even though it's still there." How many ever heard of a Christian stepping back into the old creation? If it isn't there, what did he step into? We don't have to step there; we don't have to live there. We have a new creation. How many ever have some haunting memories of what lived in that old creation? Even in the new creation, however, we aren't born complete in all its perfection. We are born with all the glorious potential.

We are creatures of an entirely different world. Don't fuddle with this old person. This new creature is only built under the dynamic of the power of the Spirit.

Detach yourself from the thing you were, and attach yourself to the new creation.

The "mixed multitude" which tagged along with the Israelites out of Egypt, and murmured in the wilderness, represents all the entanglements that impede our progress in the Spirit, and should be dropping off.

CHAPTER XXVIII

OVERCOMING

An overcomer is one that comes over and not around the difficulty.

I want the theory that disciplines me most thoroughly, and demands of me all that it possibly can; not one that makes it all so easy that there is no overcoming necessary in me; that does not minister anything to me.

There is a time to resist evil; that makes us strong in faith. There is a time, though, when He says to resist not evil, because He has permitted it to teach us how to overcome.

You say, "I want to be a real strong Christian for the Lord! I want to be all God would have me to be, I want to be an overcomer for Him in this world!" The

Lord says, "That's good, I'll accept you as a candidate." Well then what happens? He is going to send you to the school of the Spirit. He sends us to the school for our training and education. He does all that for our welfare, for our education, for our well-being. Now we have to learn to overcome. Well then, do I have to overcome something big? No, you have to overcome something small. The Holy Spirit takes you in hand and through a process of discipline and training and education you are going to learn to overcome. If you can't get the victory over something mundane, you need not worry about being a great overcomer and knowing the things of God and a deep relationship with Him.

CHAPTER XXIX

PRAYER

Touch Him when you don't know how to read the Bible, but touch the Word—touch Him; know His will; know God; know His purpose. Keep up a wonderful fellowship with the Son of God.

You can read a lot of books on prayer, some of which are quite materialistic, but no one has a form of prayer which is adequate for you. Every soul has to develop, and work out his own technique and method of prayer. Don't try to work it out by somebody else's method—it is good only for suggestions. We learn to pray by praying. We can't change God by prayer. Prayer never made God do anything. Prayer helps us become more adjusted to His will.

Look at Jesus; talk to Him; if you dare to, be informal with Him. Don't be stilted and pray, "Oh,

Thou, My God!" You can't get very far that way. How many know He is very real; very tender. Do you know that the best prayers you ever prayed never had words in them? They are so clumsy; they don't have words, because there is an understanding there; a deep, lovely, rich, inner fellowship that needs no words.

We don't know prayer: the vocal prayers, and prayers of contemplation, all the different types of prayers. It is such a vast field! We just go clattering along, saying the best we can . . . "for Jesus' sake, Amen!" To me it's such a lovely, open field we ought to get into.

He loves His children, but some don't know who they are, or what He is doing; they don't seem to know the basic, simple things that He is doing. These people know that prayer does things, so they use that as a weapon for everything under the sun, but there are a lot of things that just prayer won't do. It means a terrific lot of intelligent cooperation with Him. We can pray our heads off, but if we don't have the prayers channeled properly, with correct motivation, prayers are just like a lot of wings.

What prayers are answered? Prayers that fall into the category of the will of God. We can pray all we want to, but John says, "When we pray according to the will of God He heareth us."

Now there is this: if we will persist, God has a permissive will which He will allow. If we keep teasing, and teasing, there is a permissive will of God which He will let us have if we persist, but He will send leanness to our souls. We have no growth; no blessing; no reward, but we will have our desire, and as a result, we will have leanness in our souls. So, we have the will of God; the permissive will of God; the good will of God; the good and perfect will of God. These are all degrees of the will of God in this operation. The best thing to do is to submit it to Him. (Rom. 12:2)

In the end, all that great big prayer has to be censored in the will of God. The Holy Spirit prays according to His will.

Jesus said, "Peter, Satan hath desired to sift you . . ." This should actually read: "Satan hath obtained permission of God to sift you—all of you, but I'll stay over here and pray for you:" Don't pray now, and ask the Lord to kill the devil. He is going to use him. On the power of Jesus' prayer, Peter got through.

Prayer is never wrestling with God, but wrestling with the powers of darkness. The "unjust judge" is not a picture of God. Our heavenly Father wants to answer us; His whole heart wants to bless us. He is not the "unjust judge". (Luke 18:1-8)

Another prayer pattern we find, is the man asking for bread at midnight. (Luke 11:5-10) Sometimes we have to ask many times before the answer comes, but we must ask in faith. Hungry? He doesn't tease us; He feeds us.

Jesus prayed because He had to, to keep that contact with the Father.

"I pray for them; I pray not for the world, but for them which Thou hast given Me; for they are Thine." (John 17:9) I said, "Why Lord, isn't your great intercessory work for all those sinners out there?" He said, "For this reason. The sinner must come under the power of My redemption before he is a fit subject for My intercessions. My intercession covers those who have already been brought through the redeeming processes. Those who have not yet accepted My redemption, have no access to My prayer, but as soon as they have come through My redeeming processes, they become a subject of My intercessions."

That is why He said those strange words: "I pray not for the world—I have died for them—and if they can't come in under My death, what do My prayers mean for them? I can't do more than die! If they will come under My death purposes, then they will become subject to My prayers. So, I pray not for them—let them take the good of My death; then they will be accepted for My prayers, and I will intercede for them."

Think of Jesus interceding for us this morning before we got out of our beds! That is how I wrote that hymn: "My High Priest is Interceding for Me." He said to me, "You have faith that I am your Savior, so if you have faith in Me as your High Priest, My intercessory prayer will carry you."

There is no prayer just like intercessory prayer. It is not saying prayers; nor is it just weeping, but He says, "With groanings that we can't utter." It is past words. Why? Because the Holy Ghost makes intercession in us, and through us according to the will of God, and we can't make Him do anything else than that. We are yielded as an instrument; the Holy Ghost is praying—we aren't praying. He has a vehicle that is pliable, surrendered, and He comes in and takes possession of us. Isn't it sweet how He dares to do that? Very costly, and terrifying at times, but it's real. How is this intercessory prayer formed? It is formed according to the will of God, "with groanings which cannot be uttered"; it cannot be expressed in our language; not even with tongues, because it becomes too intense. For whom is this intercession made? It is made for the saints.

Did you ever have the Holy Spirit moving through you? What did He say? I haven't the slightest idea. He speaks secrets to the Lord. That's scriptural. I don't have to have an interpretation of what the Holy Ghost is saying to God through me. We don't have to have an interpretation every time He speaks through us. It is unto the Lord.

PRAYER: In the next age Thou wilt give us a name; help us to spell it now, Lord. Oh, grant that, by Thy Spirit, Thou shalt find it etched upon our immortal spirits, long after these fading, little bodies have gone, and we move into a new age with Thee; for what Thou has accomplished here, will reflect through the ages to come.

Did you ever try to put yourself in somebody else's place to get his reactions? You haven't lived long in God unless you can dare to do that. Most people are too egocentric; tied within the confines of their own little life, and it's impossible for them to sense how another person might feel, because they are wrapped up in the big I, ME, and MY.

If they would get out of themselves and over in the other person's situation, and feel what they feel for a little while, there would be some charity released; some love would flow. But when people haven't any sense when the love should flow; there is none. When we become identified with that awful, desperate need over there, the love of God flows right to it. In Hebrews 13:3, it says: "When ye pray, (real prayer), pray as though you were bound with the one you are praying for." But we pray 'nice' prayers!

Did you ever get into the agony of prayer when you were identified with another's need? That is intercessory prayer. We, in the Spirit, become identified with a need until we are united with it, or with a soul, or with a condition. No one in the flesh can pray a prayer like that. This is where intercessory prayer comes in. The Holy Spirit can pray prayers like that, because we can't. He wants the vehicle; He wants the instrument tied up with the condition. That is real intercessory prayer.

There are all kinds of prayer. The best prayers never have words.

CHAPTER XXX

REALM OF SPIRIT

The most real thing in the world is a life in the Spirit; that spirit open, as a sensitized plate that's exposed continually to God. Then that application of God, flowing and moving over us continually, does something to this plate. It has the power to capture, to hold, and to retain after it has been moving. Finally, we will find a deposit there—not tomorrow, or the next day. We may not find some of the reaction of these movings of God for six months, or a year, but this has been a time of His visitation. He desires the flow of that Spirit continually over us to bring the deposit of God-likeness: of Spirit and Reality in our inner consciousness of life. I believe He will do this so that we won't be the same any more.

People are utterly starved to death. For what? Food; not milk, but for some meat, and some strong meat. They need it; they need it badly. God can't take a Body that is just a whimpering baby to sit on the throne with Him and share—He can't do things like that. There will be a place for babes; I imagine heaven will have a tremendously large nursery!

Many have never come into an inner consciousness of a birth; it is a potential matter with them. We are birthed into a vast realm. When we say "kingdom", then right away we are thinking of horses, bugles, and banners, but it is a vast field; a realm. When He was talking about coming into the kingdom, He was not talking about heaven. He called the kingdom a vast realm.

Now by the power of the Spirit, He will gradually bring us into an inner consciousness of that realm; maybe not the first day, nor the first year. I have had to deal with souls who have been filled with the Spirit ten, twenty years, who have not yet come into the consciousness of that! Now what is in this realm? All spiritual reality.

In the natural, there are laws which He has established for our well-being in order that we can live a comfortable life. It would be a great aid to us if we would discover the laws in the realm of Spirit, and come under the power of the laws which God has placed there.

He doesn't want us so super doodle in the Spirit that we can't know beans from buttons. He wants us perfectly practical, and able to discern that, and yet all the time saying, "That is not my realm; that natural realm is not my realm. Here is my realm; I live with Him in spirit." Now in this spiritual realm I have been making discoveries of truths, principles, laws, methods, and facts which are just as real as those in the natural realm, but they are abstract, and spiritual. Therefore, most people never bother with them at all.

Of course, if you want to live on that natural plane, live on it; go to heaven, and play on a harp. But you will never yet find the thing that God intended us to have in the Spirit. In that spiritual realm I make discoveries; I find how God works; I watch Him work here; watch Him work there, and then as I go around in the Word, I see it. I am like a hound dog in the Word. Sometimes I am in it a year, sometimes two, chasing that Truth down; and so I make my discoveries.

He didn't bring in the kingdom then, but He introduced a brand new order—not an earthly kingdom, but a life in the Spirit.

In Luke 24:13-35, we read of Emmaus; the house by the side of the road. This little cottage is our inner chamber, the inner recesses of this strange creature that you and I are. On the dusty road of escapism He expounded to the two disciples the Truth, but though their hearts burned within them; their eyes were not yet opened as to Who He really was. They had not yet come into the proper place for the unveiling. He was waiting to bring the revelation to its consummation, but He couldn't do it on the dusty road while they were reasoning in their agitated hearts—not even in the presence of the exposition of Truth which made their hearts burn. But when they constrained Him to come into the inner recesses of their being—their whole soul and being—He went in. The door was closed to every external contact with which they had thus far been familiar.

The breaking of bread was an old custom; it was a covenant that one entered into for fellowship. Our life is a loaf of bread. He takes the bread, worships, breaks it, and gives it back to us. His hands have received it; His hands have touched it, and we will never live the same again. He is made known to us as to the two disciples in the breaking of our hearts and lives; He is unveiled to us through that. We heard Him; we saw Him; we had an inner vision of Him, but now we KNOW Him.

We learn the laws of living in the realm of spiritual reality, by living.

Education is good, but I want it to be where it belongs. It is the mechanism, the mechanics, the world of flesh and time. It does not belong in the realm of Spirit. Therefore, the things of the Spirit of God are not known, nor understood by these mechanics. They cannot be; they are diametrically opposed.

CHAPTER XXXI

REDEMPTION

Paul, with regard to his body, spoke of its majesty as a "temple of God", a sacred, wonderful thing. Paul gave it the elevation it needed. "Know ye not that ye are the temple of God?" He will dwell in it, and there will be temple worship. He will dwell in us; He will sing in us; He will have real temple worship, because we are a temple of the Holy Ghost. God let me see that picture to show me the dignity of the body as a temple.

Now look at another picture. Peter talked about the body as "a little collapsible tent" in which we live. Note the contrast between the two: the majesty in one; the frailty in the other. In Scripture our bodies are called "tabernacles," but in Greek the word means "a little collapsible tent". It is a limited thing. But, if this little collapsible tent falls down and perishes, that is not the end! We have a dwelling place with God in the heavenlies, for we shall always have a habitat.

Now remember, in the scheme of redemption, redemption will cover all these features: spirit, soul, body. How do we know the body is included? In the redemptive scheme of God, even our bodies which are laid to rest upon Old Mother Earth are included, and she opens her arms and puts us to sleep in them. I am never afraid of the grave—never think of it. I shall be happy to go back to my Old Mother Earth. I like my Mother Earth. She has given me what I have. Everything I have of this physical has come out of the earth. So I wrote a little poem about it and I call it:

"Recompense"

Give me of thyself, O gentle earth, Food for my body while I live.

We have much in common, you and I, You kept me living since my birth.

Some day in return to you I'll give Dust of my body—when I die.

I offer back to Mother Earth this instrument that she has built for me, and I say, "I am all through with it, Mother Earth, I give it back to thee,"—recompense. I always feel as if Mother Earth opens her arms and puts me to sleep against her breast. Grave? Oh, no, don't say that! Will redemption come? Yes, He will even bring bodies that have been laid away under the redemptive work of Christ, and we will have a resurrection. So you see the redemption of Christ comes even after the body is disposed of. The body too shall have the power of redemption, and it shall be changed and glorified. This is the work of the Holy Spirit.

God slew an animal. In Genesis 3:21 we read: ". . . the Lord God made coats of skins, and clothed them." The skin is inclusive; everything in us is inside the skin. Biologically, skin holds all that there is of us. He showed me that it was an inclusive redemption. The skin includes the whole redemption process. All that there was of the animal was hidden away in the skin. He says, "I'll give the skin, the all-over, the whole inclusive covering of the redemption of Christ", and He covers them.

You can't exhaust the triumph and the victory of the Calvary experience; the redemption of His universe and the putting it back in order. You can push out the redemption as far as you want to; it covers.

Redemption brings us into great privileges. It brings us into the intercessions of Christ, and into the image of Christ, which is His supreme objective.

To me redemption is for Him to revolutionize us; overhaul us; revive and possess us, so that in every field He will have the dominion, and the right, and the way.

CHAPTER XXXII

RESURRECTION

The resurrection of Jesus was God's seal and act of approval signifying that His death was sufficient. Jesus never resurrected Himself—God raised Him from the dead. God the Father was pleased, and satisfied with His victorious life and death. In raising Him from the dead, God gave testimony that all was satisfactory.

In 1 Corinthians 15, Paul, in speaking of the resurrection, says, "I will show you a mystery." He didn't say, "I will define it, or explain it." As there are so many different glories of stars, SO is the resurrection of the dead! Everyone will be raised according to his own rank and glory. There is classification and order.

Concerning resurrection, we read in Hebrews 11:35b: ". . . others were tortured, not accepting deliverance, that they might obtain a better resurrection." Those who have suffered correctly are waiting for a better resurrection.

In Acts 1:8, the Lord is not using the word "witness" about someone who gets up and gives a testimony; He is saying that a person coming up from the power of the Spirit, is willing to let his life be slain in order that the life of the Christ may be lived through him. He becomes a witness, a testimony of the power of God. That is when the individual life becomes a witness; a testimony. The word "witness" here means "martyr"; one who is willing to let his very life go for the sake of the Truth.

The power of His resurrection possessed the disciples, and the power of the resurrection is always a witnessing power. The resurrection was a witness. The power that God used in raising Jesus from the dead was resurrection power unto a witness. When does He say, "I will pour the Holy Spirit upon you"? After the resurrection, for now there is resurrection quality in the power that is to come upon them. They are now ministering in resurrection power. The LIFE is the witness.

The bread and wine sacrament is a type of regeneration and resurrection. These emblems decompose, ferment, speaking of death. Then comes a higher form of life both in the bread and wine. The process is the same in both. In the bread we have the yeast, the leaven, which speaks of sin. This is no longer active as it decomposes, and is changed. In the wine there is also fermentation—death. It has no longer form as before.

On the seventh month, the seventeenth day of the month, the ark rested on Ararat. This is the anniversary of the resurrection!

CHAPTER XXXIII

SATAN

When the devil looked at Calvary, he saw his Waterloo—his defeat. That's what the matter with him is. The devil is conscious of his defeat. That is why, in the closing of this dispensation, the wrath of the enemy is being felt all the time in more intense form, because he sees the net drawing in. In the end, he will become fairly frantic. He will possess, and move through every instrument he can find, in politics, in society, in art and music, in every form that he can get in. In the last days he is going to be captured in his own net. He sees his utter defeat at Calvary.

A demon is as evasive and subtle as a snake.

I never reason with the devil. He is unreasonable.

The devil is a servant, after all, and God uses him when He wants to. With Paul, He let a demon loose, "a messenger of Satan to buffet him."

CHAPTER XXXIV

SECOND COMING

In regard to the Second Coming, the believer does not need the external signs such as the Jew returning to Israel. Those are for the ones who need to be aroused by great signs—but the believer is looking for these spiritual signs:

1. When the cup of iniquity is full. (That's the negative sign.)

2. When the Bride has made herself ready. (That's the positive sign.)

"Behold, I come quickly: hold that fast which thou hast, that no man take thy crown." (Rev. 3:11) "I come quickly" —not in the sense of time, but in the manner—like a flash; "That no man take thy crown"— in the sense of a bird snatching the seed (Truth) as in the parable of the sower; (Mark 4:4) "Hold fast the Truth—keep and guard My Word and message; hold; grasp the deposit of Truth, for it relates to a crown ("That no man take thy crown").

CHAPTER XXXV

SPIRITUAL DEVELOPMENT

I keep warning young people, and I often say to them, "Listen, this is the only time you will have to make certain decisions, surrenders, and choices in your life. These decisions and choices that you make now govern marvelously things which will happen thousands of years in the next age. This is the period in which you make the choice; not the period in which it is going to be exhausted. After you are released, and you are on the other side, you can't come back here, and make the choices you should make now. This is the period in which He plows the heart, which is like a plot of ground, with the Word, which is the Eternal Truth."

The plowshare is the Eternal Truth that tears my inner heart and life; and exposes it to the sun and air. Truth plows us; we have to be plowed before He can even sow the seed. He plows; then He sows the seed. He only gives it a little while to root, and push through, enough to give identification. It pushes up through the soil of my whole life, and shows what it is. I will have the eternal ages for it to mature; to grow; to glorify God, and to live.

Life is projected upon planes. We are on a journey back home to the heart of God where we belong. We don't belong here. We are only here for a period of training and culture; a little period of spiritual exercise to bring adjustment in spiritual living, which may be projected upon another plane in ages yet to come.

This little period we call time is just a little probation time in which we are able to make the elementary and fundamental adjustments of spiritual living. That is all we can hope to do here. There is not too much maturity. The real, vital thing He is after, is a spiritual adjustment to reality; a spiritual conception of Truth and God. It takes some years to reach His objective. Don't expect it in a minute. There will be something of the life of Christ in us that can adapt itself to another age.

Why not learn the voice of God; we have to live with it the rest of our lives. Why not take a little time to be keen enough to detect His leadings, and know the whispers of the Spirit; know the intimation of the Spirit in our inner being. It need not be in words—just that strange, mystical, impact of Spirit in us that knows. We are to develop that. Take time to learn how to do that, because that is living, and that is living in the Spirit. We can't get it in a minute. There are no short-cuts, and there are no gadgets with buttons we can press so that out pops the answer. This miserable way we have today: press a button, and that comes on, and press a button, and on and on . . . What a way to live! No originality in it; no loveliness of your own life coming through. It is a mechanical sort of riggamaroo, I don't like it.

We take that sort of a thing right into the Spirit, and we think that we are going to get things from God that way, and that we are going to overcome that way, and we begin to live in the Spirit that way, but we can't. We just can't.

The life in the Spirit holds a lot of drudgery. But if we become keen enough to detect His leadings, then when tragedy comes we have the consciousness of this inner life; the Presence of the Lord; the voice of God; the courage of the Spirit. Take time out to learn these elementary things consisting of the power of the Word, and Truth, because that is what we have to live by as we move on.

I want you to have the Truth, and when God begins to deal with you and me to accomplish in us these lovely things which will pass through time into the ages yet to come, let us not be fearful, let us not be afraid. We are in the hands of the living God, and He will see us through. "He Who hath begun a good work in you will also finish it." Let Him finish it!

Just as soon as the ground is fairly settled, and in any way comfortable, He will put His Truth in there and plow it all up again. He doesn't want it settled and static.

"And when His disciples, James and John, saw this (that they would not receive Him) they said, Lord, wilt Thou that we command fire to come down from heaven, and consume them, even as Elias did? But he turned, and rebuked them, and said, Ye know not what manner of spirit ye are of." (Luke 9:54, 55) The difficulty with the disciples was not in love, or in power, but in spirit. The territory that yet has to be discovered in my heart sometimes amazes me! Did you ever feel that there is territory in you that has to be taken yet; possessed by Him? Sure, there are territories in my being that I have not become conscious of, but God knows, and I know that He has to triumph in those fields. He has to go in and make conquest in the territories of this creature.

I accept the discipline, and trying things He tosses into my pattern. They are so necessary. They are not punishment for failure, or sin, but the only means He has of developing us. Never let the devil get you down when God is working in and for you.

Jesus grew, and He learned through a law of suffering. We can grow just as much as we want to, and we can learn lust as much as we want to. It takes a lifetime. (Heb. 5:8; 2:10) This is my little schoolroom down here, called "time"—a little segment of the eternal circle. This is my period of discovery, education, training, etc. We don't have to do a lot of research work; get a little from this or that; we remain with Him Who IS THE TRUTH. There are vast fields of Truth yet to be ventured upon. We must go in. My emphasis is on learning how to live.

He launches us into a new realm of spiritual reality, called "kingdom." Jesus uses the word "realm" instead of "kingdom." I like that better—a vast realm. We have all the eternal ages into which this light and Truth can be projected.

When the Holy Spirit begins to work with you, offer to Him, with all the abandonment that you have; that aptitude; that urge; just that little flickering hunger for more of God—cultivate that. That is, to me, the choicest thing there is in us. Why? Because it is the root of all the possibilities in the ages to come. They are hidden potentially in that little, quivering urge in your heart. That's true. All that we will carry over into the next realm is the amount of spiritual life; understanding; spiritual opening; yieldedness; awareness; the amount of that spiritual life that we have; that's what we carry over into the next age. God begins to work with us from that angle. When we are translated, or brought into heaven, we are not matured. He takes us exactly where we are now in our spiritual development. If we are a babe in Christ, translation never makes us into a matured saint; neither does death, because God has a law that governs in that field, just as much as in the field of gravitation. That's scriptural.

This little hunger that is in our heart—this little urge—has to be trained, and educated. The fact that we are brought into heaven doesn't mature us. We have all the eternal ages in which we may grow in God. Why? Because He is Infinite. Do you think we are going to get to the end of Infinity? We can't exhaust it; neither can we exhaust the revelation of light and Truth that shines in God—the Ancient of Days. This is the little conception we have of Him here in time, but what will be the conception when we move out of time?

When Jesus takes us home, all we will take with us is what we have acquired here of spiritual value. This is a little time of schooling. Don't become too satisfied with the seat that you are holding in school while you are being taught; (your automobile, your house, how many dollars, a name, a reputation); it all goes to the wind like that! He doesn't consider it. That has been the mechanics which operated in your heart and life while you, as a dynamic spirit; a conscious entity; born of God; filled with Him; illuminated by Him, are pushing your way through; pushing your way through to where? Home, back to God; this should be your attitude.

CHAPTER XXXVI

SPIRITUAL FOOD

". . . Lord, feed me with food convenient for me." (Prov. 30:8b) People are choosy, they want the things they want. They may not need a thrill; they may need a pill! A child can't diagnose his need; the wise parent has to feed him. ". . . Lord feed me with food convenient, (or even better) food which is my allotment, or my portion." When we pray that, we take our hands off the table, and put them under it! (I am very polite; my hands are under the table!) Sometimes He gives us a portion we don't like, but it will do us good. Cultivate your appetite.

The children of Israel, in the wilderness, "gathered Manna, every man according to his eating"—his capacity. (Ex. 16:18) How much have you gathered this day; enough to slake your hunger? There is enough for the thimble capacity, and the dishpan capacity. It is readily available; close at hand; at your tent door. Some of you are looking for Manna without a night.

It comes to my "dust" (my humanity).

CHAPTER XXXVII

SPIRITUAL LAWS

I want to help you so that when trouble comes, or when you have difficulties, you will not cast away your faith, but be able to have it stabilized in God, and take of the grace of God, which He has freely given, and does give to tide us along. I want you to have some of these basic Truths in your hearts and minds, and be able to apply, what I call Christian philosophy, to your daily walk.

If we can do that, we get through. But if we are ignorant of the ways of life, and the laws and principles which God has given us, our lives become sometimes quite tragic. This need not be. Even though tragedy may come as a means of discipline to us, He gives us power and grace to interpret it, so that it doesn't leave a scar and mar our spirits. We receive it; get our discipline out of it, and what God wants; then lay it aside as some accommodation which He gave. "That was a tragedy that soured my life;" we say, "and I'll never be the same." Don't do that. That is a very strange and wrong reaction. MEET IT!

As a child of God, I have come back to my Paradise place, where God is responsible for my wherewithal. God was responsible when He made Adam, but Adam, as a creature, didn't like God's way of managing. Now he is dead spiritually, and by the sweat of his brow, he has to get out under the burden of living—see if you can "pay your taxes . . ."

God cursed the EARTH. What good would it have done to curse a dead man? The earth now resists man. So many of us that have come back to God—to our original place—having been lighted; (for "he has lighted my candle" Psa. 18:28) have been able to sense that He is all we need.

As a real child of God, we have come back again to the first place, and position in Him where God provides. Paul says so;—even if it is just clothes and fish, God will provide. He likes to because we are His children. I think He likes to do it, but He is also obligated to! Why? Because we have met a law of spiritual adjustment, in the realm of the Spirit. It was about the very first thing Jesus taught the disciples: "If you seek first the kingdom of God and His righteousness, all these things shall be added unto you." (Matt. 6:33)

A life is not safe in itself unless it is surrendered to God. Neither are the things which He permits or brings to us, unless they first go through His hands. That is why He calls us so many times to surrender certain things to Him, and we have a terrific time, as we say, dying our death and surrendering the things to God. That is necessary, but it isn't because He wants them. They can't enrich Him; they can't make Him more God because of it. The enrichment comes back as a reflex in us, because we have surrendered them. That which is most choice must be surrendered to Him to its death so that it can come back again safe and sound in its resurrection—in time, when we are ready. He only wants them in His hands: the cleansing medium. We bring the quivering sacrifice which is torn from our hearts, and we think we will die because of it, and we put it with trembling hands into the hands of God. He says, "Thank you." Now that kiss of God upon the sacrifice takes the danger element out of it, and when He gives it back it is safe. Sometimes, though, He keeps it.

So if He sees it is wholesome for us to have it, He cancels the danger point by bringing us to a place of surrender where we can allow it to go to its death. Then He says, "Thank you, I don't want it, really, you can have it." Unless it goes through His hands first, it is still a dangerous element for us to have. Paul, in order to actually maintain what God desired in his pattern, had to SUFFER the loss to make it good. "If there be first a "willing spirit" over a situation, IT (that willing spirit) is accepted as though the whole deed were done. To one He says, "You are not safe with it; it is not good for you; you give that to Me." To another He says, "I can trust you with it. I have not come to rob; I have come to give LIFE—and that more abundantly."

Too many interests are detrimental to real spiritual life.

All ministry, whether we are preaching or teaching, or whatever our vocation, which is in the will of God, is purely reactionary. It is not to get something done; it is to get something done in you, and in me through the media of our immediate task. God is after you, and after me first. He lets us ride along quite a long time, and then: woe to the flesh; woe to the old creation; woe to this old ego. But I tell you something, there will be life, life, life, but it has to come through that process. Through the ministries and service which is given to us, we are changed, released, and conformed to the image of Christ.

To the disciples, who were under a tradition of a King, quarreling about reigning and ruling over this city and that city, He would say, "Don't be too sure about that. Have you exhausted the study of a Paschal Lamb? Do you know all that pertains to the Lamb before you get so intrigued about reigning and ruling?"

That Kingship will come, but we surely have to know a Lamb before we know a King—a Lamb that taketh away the sin of the world. How liberating that is; how broad; what a universal thing!

"Behold the Lamb of God that taketh away the sin of the world." Someday it will be: "Behold the Bridegroom cometh." You will never have a Bridegroom without a Lamb.

Life only comes through death. That is a spiritual law. Character takes time to build, under a law of testing and proving.

God works with indirect methods; not from frontal attacks. In Paul's time, as now, the world was just as rotten everywhere. We don't find him making a direct attack on one of those existing conditions. It has to come indirectly through the life of the individual. "Overcome evil by good"—and good is the life manifested continually in such an individual, overpowering the other. But you can't legislate it. It is slow, but it is His way.

Peter and all the rest of the disciples were fishing all night in disobedience after Jesus' crucifixion. Jesus knew every nail in the boat, and every scale on the fish. Jesus saith unto them, "Children, have ye any meat?" (John 21:5) He wasn't asking for information at all. Why was He asking? Here we have a little principle: a question asked, provokes an answer. The answer becomes the platform upon which the blessing is released.

"Have ye any fish?"

"No."

"No" is one of the most difficult words to pronounce in the English language!

The two disciples on the Road to Emmaus had sold out everything. They had followed Him, but didn't get Him on the throne. They loved the Lord, but they loved their own lives too. They were afraid of losing their investment, and so, when He spoke of death, Calvary: "I must go"—they didn't want that.

They wanted a kingdom. But He died! He was not going to make a kingdom. The kingdom had become a fixation in them. The resurrection was the most profound thing that had happened. Do you think that moved them? No, not at all. The very last question those disciples ever asked the Lord, after the tragedy of Calvary, and the miracle of the resurrection, was: "When wilt Thou restore the kingdom?" Even that marvelous resurrection did not budge the fixation. It still held until the very hour He was taken up. They still grab at His garments and ask, "Will we now have a kingdom?"

I think those are the most tragic words in the New Testament as far as the disciples are concerned. What a picture of their attitude of heart! He has a marvelous Substitute, (the Holy Spirit), but if we are not willing to wait for the revelation of a Substitute, we move out under a poor premise, and collapse. Peter went back, (they all did), to the nets. Misery loves company. One disciple could not bear it alone. When we fail in the Spirit, we always react in the natural. If we can't move in the power of the Spirit, in faith, we will revert to the natural—it is a law.

The law for building the temple— the building which we are—is testing and proving. He has no other way. It is an established law by which we grow.

Salvation is a gift; the baptism of the Spirit is purely on the gift level; healing is on a gift level; all those lovely, elementary things, the first principles which are presented to us at the base of our mountain climb, all those are purely on the basis of gifts. But we cannot remain there, and be on the mountain. Paul says, "Leaving behind; forgetting; dropping these 'elementary' first principles, (not in the sense of value, but in their position). Don't forsake them; don't belittle them; don't throw them out the window; let them be exactly where they are, but "Let us go on to completion." (Heb. 6:1) How will we get there? A law works right away. We will never get away from it; we might just as well own and accept it. If you have to quarrel, go to the Lord with your quarrel, and say, "Lord, You could have made it easier."—A stone has to be chiseled and hammered before it can be put in the building. (Eph. 2:19, 20, 22)

A spiritual need cannot be satisfied by a natural application, as was the case with Adam and Eve making aprons. Man has a material outlook today, extremely too much so; so that he has very little appreciation or understanding, not only of spiritual things pertaining to God, but of spiritual values in the world. We know there are spiritual values in the world, as well as spiritual values in God. We fall back upon nature to supply a spiritual need. Wherever there is a spiritual need, nature always comes in, though broken down, trying to remedy it. "That which is spiritual is not first, but natural, afterward that which is spiritual." (1 Cor. 15:46) Man (the flesh) has to have a fling at the natural first, as shown in the disciples first counting the bread and fish, and in Adam bringing out a natural display of fig leaves. First the natural, fig leaves, then the spiritual, a lamb.

Don't be afraid of your limitations (five loaves, two fishes). Let God get hold of them; put your limitations in the hands of the Miracle Worker. Five thousand are fed and blessed!

CHAPTER XXXVIII

SUFFERING

Suffering brings us into the fellowship of the Trinity:

1. Father—Disciplines us as sons, and we recognize Him as our heavenly Father. Discipline entails or spells suffering, which is necessary and needed; otherwise we are bastards.

2. Son—Jesus, as Son of Man, learned obedience by the things He suffered. So will we as He conforms us to his image. Again, this entails suffering.

3. Holy Spirit—We will suffer in our spirit. Jesus suffered in His spirit. The physical suffering really is nothing compared to what the spirit suffers.

He is a suffering God—a God of love, but a suffering God. So we, as cells in that Body, partake of the same. There are hidden treasures in Christ; He is a wonderful Redeemer, but He is a suffering Redeemer. The Body is being formed and shaped, and we are the cells, and members. This Body will have to partake of the same characteristics that we find in our wonderful Lord.

Paul said, "I die daily." Paul knew something of the program of God.

There is no getting into God without suffering. In school, there is no education without studying. Without discipline, there is no getting into God. Obedience—we never know real obedience unless we know these three: suffering, discipline, obedience. They, as the media by which we enter into God, are interrelated.

In our hearts, we feel perfectly sure He is right in permitting the suffering, though we cannot answer the "why" every time. "When I came into the house of the Lord, I understood." We will have a spiritual consciousness of reality and Truth; it does not come by natural reasoning. Where revelation ceases, speculation begins. I can give as my personal testimony that these deeper revelations of Truth, and clear understanding of the things of God, have come only through suffering.

CHAPTER XXXIX

TEACHERS

The reason why Paul taught as earnestly as he did, was because his great field was that of a teacher. He was a missionary—that was the external manifestation of the work which he did, but underneath all of that, there was the most profound urge and drive in that man as a teacher; absolutely!

What did those early teachers teach? They introduced the people into a new realm of Spirit with contact with God. The Jews hadn't had that in the old order. Teachers were chosen, illuminated spirits, with personality gifts; illuminated in the field of spiritual reality. Their ministry was to bring from that field the knowledge, the Truth, the revelation; all that would feed this Body; instruct it; give it its place.

CHAPTER XL

TEACHING

"Train up a child in the way he should go: and when he is old, he will not depart from it." (Prov. 22:6) I have learned a lot of things you parents don't know. Your proximity hinders you. Does it say 'tell' a child what he should do, and when he is old, he will not depart from it? It does not say 'tell' a child, for you can tell a child ten thousand times, but the telling has to take another step. It is not in the telling. If you tell Tommy to do something, and he doesn't do it, see to it that he does, even if you have to let the beans burn on the stove. You told him a hundred times, but you didn't see to it that he did it once! See to it that he does it the once. It will save you the ninety-nine times. Take time.

Here are the three "T's":

TELL, TEACH, TRAIN.

He moves from the first "T" which is to tell; then he must be taught the thing which has been told him. The telling is not the teaching. Did you give him a lesson in the things you told him? Some day he will be really vexed with you because you didn't teach him. He will say, "Why didn't you ever correct me on that?" After he has been taught the thing which he has been told, he has to be trained in the thing, In other words, he has to be trained in the thing he has been taught, in the thing he has been told, by everlasting drilling, and training, which should follow the lesson, which has been once learned; or else he will have lost the application, if he has not been drilled, and trained in the lesson which he first learned.

God's method is the same in the school of the Holy Spirit. He takes us up, as pliable material, to build personalities in God; men and women in God who know spiritual life and values, The HOLY SPIRIT dwells in us as a great Tutor Who instructs us in the great university.

A pianist first has to be told a lot. He may have the potential possibilities first, but all the knowledge which he has about that music, doesn't make him a great pianist. It gives him the equipment necessary, but all the lovely values have never come out yet. He must learn by a lesson, and be taught the scales first. Then he has to be drilled and trained in the lesson he has learned.

The word education comes from: e = "out, evacuate," duco = "to leave"; acqua = "velvet water, smooth, aqueduct, watering duct, leading out into". He is not educated until that knowledge has come down into livable portions. How does he know how to act in certain circumstances? Education is to "lead out." It is unto a purpose. He has his head all filled with a lot of facts, but he is not yet educated. That which he has received has never acquired an adequate expression in life. Education involves a process. The telling; the lessons; growth; training involves doing and executing.

Telling is the storing up; teaching, its power; training makes the doing substance; "that he can't depart from it." It makes it a part of his life; there is no separation. It is a part of him. It is not something he heard, for he can slip away from that. If he doesn't learn his lessons faithfully, he forgets them. So training is unto the doing—the application.

Jesus went up and down the country telling the good news. He told everybody; multitudes heard Him, but all the multitudes, having heard that glorious Truth, were not wonderful spiritual people just because they were told. "He spoke not to the multitude but by a parable." They had the multitude power, capacity, and receptivity. But when He was alone, "He expounded all things to His disciples." A disciple is a taught-one. All Christians who are saved are not disciples. A disciple requires qualification. ". . . And seeing the multitude, He said: If any man will be My disciple, let him deny himself and take up his cross and follow Me." Take up the cross which will kill the old creation, lest it would hinder the new creation.

Disciples are called-out ones from the believing multitude; they are taught and disciplined. They can be disciplined in very many measures aside from using a stick! "For whom the Lord loveth He chasteneth, child-trains, and scourgeth every son whom He receiveth." (Heb. 12:6)—(See also Prov. 15:5, 31, 32; 13:18-24; 19:1-8; 22:15; 23:12, 14; 29:15)

CHAPTER XLI

TESTING AND PROVING

I always deal with God. I never deal with the devil. We say: "I defy the devil!" It takes the LORD to rebuke him! He is loose, but God is back of him. I get right behind Jesus; He is my Elder Brother. He will take me through, and He is my glorious High Priest who intercedes for me. I am conscious of the devil, but I know better than to get into a squabble with him.

My garden has something besides roses in it. It has a tree of the knowledge of good and evil, and a serpent. God had to have the tree, because He is building a man. Who takes possession of the tree? The enemy does tempting to divert us. In the Name of Jesus, refuse it! Character is built through a law of testing and proving. Nature is a gift. We have to do with the shaping of character, but we don't have to do with the nature that God gave us. Accept the law of testing and proving if the life of Christ is to be manifested. Grow like Him, and grow with Him. We are only safe when we choose the will of God.

All life, wherever it is manifested, is a manifestation of God. It may run in terrifying channels, and it may be used to horrible destruction, but every bit of life and power that is manifested, is of God. He is the one who originates life. The devil uses it, and misuses it, terrifies the world with it, and he swings it out in all kinds of fashions, but he is not the author of it, for he has life originally from God.

What would have happened if Adam and Eve had refused the subtle arguments of the enemy? They would have met another tree. Why? Because the strength of that which they had gained in the first testing would have had to go through a crucible, and come out tested. The tree was to build them, and to release, not destroy them. If they had not failed, they would have had enough trees, (testings) to do something. It would have perfected them, and brought them through to a lovely glorification, as it did the Last Adam, Jesus, on the Mt. of Transfiguration.

I want to help you with this question of trouble, trials, testings, and provings. Since our lives are full of them, we should not be disturbed if we can't pray them all out of our pattern. Because, if we are consecrated spirits, dedicated to God, He is very familiar with every bit of the paraphernalia that is thrown into our life pattern. He knows it before we do. He never permits anything to come, unless it touches Him first. Even the devil can't touch us unless God permits him. God knows all about it. That should encourage us if the testings and provings come—they have to come as a part of our economy as Christians.

I will show you a reason for the necessity of testings and provings by going back to Genesis. "And God breathed into his nostrils the breath of life." In Hebrew, "life" is plural; "lives". Why? The minute that breath of God strikes this human creature, who is made to function with God on that level, he would have that life flowing in two directions. In its first direction, it is to flow back again to God, and make this man a unit—one with God. He is created of God, and he is created for God. His life (lives) becomes a spiritual manifestation, and also a physical manifestation, and his body begins to function. His life (lives) strikes in two directions:

1.   It brings this creature into a conscious relation with God. Keep this communion open; keep that alive.

2.   It is responsive to the world, because it has the life of God in it, which brings him in contact with the physical things of this world as well.

Everything in him responds, because of the life element which sets free ten thousand things that are hidden in him. They were never, never manifested in Adam—they never had a chance, but they were there.

God made man with two trinities:

1.   Spirit, soul, body.

2.   Personality; consisting of intellectual gifts; emotional reactions; power to choose.

God is working all the time in those two trinities. We have the power of the will to choose, and character is built under a law of testing and proving.

We have no life in ourselves; we are dependent; therefore we must go daily to the Tree of Life, which symbolizes Christ. (Matt. 6:11) There are two forces in terrific conflict. The enemy hates God. He took one-third of the hosts of heaven with him. God told Adam, "This is the tree of the knowledge of good and evil; keep away from it, for in the day ye eat thereof, ye shall die. I will give you all the knowledge of good and evil that you need. I have all you need, and I will give to you. But that tree is a strange thing, and I am not explaining it to you—it is a tree symbolizing the knowledge of good and evil. I don't want you to be awakened to that. That is Satanic! For in the day that you do, you shall die."

Death was not in the thought of God at all—translation was. "You keep your power of choice in Me, and say, 'Yes' with Me." Now God planted that tree before the devil got in there. "When the power of choice comes, keep choosing with Me." Sin erased the spiritual aspect of Adam's being, and he became subnormal; psychic; intellectual, and body conscious, and the majority of people are subnormal to this day.

"In the day thou eatest thereof thou shalt surely die." Did He say: "You will go to hell?" No. We know there is hell and all that, but that isn't His proposition. He is coming to a proposition of life and death. It was an issue of life and death there in the garden. That issue has never changed. Theology changes; doctrines will change; church creeds will change; their philosophy will change, but God never changes. We go right back to the garden, and there it is; a law of testing and proving, with the issue—life and death. He still works on that basis today.

God cannot be tempted, nor does He tempt anyone. But God tests us, and proves us, because we are His workmanship; He wants to develop us, and bring us into a place of victory and life in Him. He can only do it through the law of testing. Temptation is always unto defeat and death. Testing is always unto strength and life.

Always remember when we meet this tree, we don't have a united prayer meeting where all of the saints come with their axes, all ground and sharp with the Word of God, full of faith, and they say, "Now in the name of the Lord, we will deliver this poor saint," and we chop his tree down! But they say, "The tree has the devil in it!" Well of course, where would the devil be? He's in the tree. "Oh, Lord, kill the devil." "I can't! I want him. He is My shepherd dog, he is running around after the sheep, getting them in line. I am not going to destroy the very instrument that I am using."

How will I ever get hold of Job? Can you imagine God, saying, "We'll go down tonight, and politely say, 'Dear Brother Job, there is something I have to say unto thee, and I really want you to understand this, Job . . . you are thus and so, but I think I can help you.'" How silly that would be! The Lord uses the devil to get at Job.

He says, "No tree; no temptation has beset you, but what is common to man, but God has with the tree which He has made, also made a way of escape." He makes the situation, and He makes a way of escape, but we always want a shortcut through. "He hath also with the testing made a way of escape, that ye may endure it." Through the testing, God will be glorified in us.

He can only make us mature saints through a life process. I want you to be students of the Word, students of life, and students of what God is doing; how He does it, and why He does it. Then we become what I call spiritually intelligent. Why do we have testings? Why do we have discipline? To release, and build this wonderful Christian character through our intelligent cooperation with Him, saying, "I choose with God."

I can give my whole life as a testimony of the Truth that I impart. Whoever gets anything from God without having a hard time? The great artist, Van Gogh, is an example: His Master Teacher told him, "I am glad you have to paint on an empty stomach; nothing in this world, worthwhile, has ever been done comfortably." Nothing worthwhile has ever been done comfortably, and nothing worthwhile that we have to give is due to a comfortable habit.—"Measure thy life by loss, and not by gain . . ."

Don't let the glory of this present victory blind you to what is down the road, or around the corner, because the Lord is going to test the strength of this victory. The strength of this victory will be tried out again and again and again. He tries us continually in order to develop our spiritual strength.

Usually in a test, even a long one, we become too involved and localized, and the pressure makes us so present conscious that at times we lose all sense of proportion. But after a while we get quiet, and look back, and get a perspective and view what we missed before. So I am seeing now (3 yrs. later) at least a little of why things have to come our way.

CHAPTER XLII

TRUTH

I have given out plenty of Truth, and yet some say, "Oh, give us more." What have you done with what I have already given? You enjoy the Truth, but sometimes there is a fascination in its revelation that bewitches you, and you want to know more about that, but you don't want to know about the power of its reaction in you.

That is where your trouble is. We must always remember that there is a reaction in this Truth business. We want it —that's good—the desire is there; that is wholesome. One day I said, "I want the Truth, Lord." But you see, if we really mean that, the entrance of Truth in our hearts and lives is the most disastrous thing we could ask for; that is, if we let it accomplish its features and purposes. It isn't something that liberates us, and makes us happy. That is one aspect of its reaction, but Truth, in its power, in its essence, is the most terrifying thing I have found, but I didn't know it in the beginning.

Truth has a two-fold action in us. It will begin pleasing us, of course; that is good psychology; quite agreeable; it has a great charm. We say, "Truth, how wonderful!" Now, if we embrace it; if we actually open our hearts to that, and we say, "Lord, I want the Truth," we better be very careful what we pray about. He might come in with the power of Truth. What does it do? It becomes devastating since we have to have it in this negative aspect first. Truth will slay us, because the Lord is not interested in this carnal, natural setup. It has to go by a way of death before it can be released in life. That is a law in the realm of Spirit, and the realm of Spirit is filled with laws as real as the law of gravitation.

People, however, would rather have a manifestation they can look at: grow a leg on Susie . . . see how He did that! We get caught on some item, an experience, and we cannot move. Use them as most fleeting, most fleeting; value them; appreciate them; give them their full value, but move on.

He says, "If I come in that negative power, it will slay you, but there is a reaction; I only slay that I may bring resurrection and life." So Truth will slay us, but Truth is the only medium He has for its resurrection.

I like Peter because he is aggressive, and I like John because he is a mystic. I work with all people, because Truth is too big for one church. No one has a corner on it. If I found a bunch of people who thought they had all the Truth, I'd leave them. Nobody has all the Truth; we have the Bible, but I mean the revelation of its contents.

Truth is not only objective, but when people yield their hearts and lives to the Holy Spirit, the Spirit can take this Truth, and incorporate it into their lives until the things which are purely judicial may be brought down to actual living. The Holy Spirit takes that which is purely objective and judicial, and makes it a reality in your life until it is incorporated into your being; it will then be a subjective realization.

SUBJECTIVE—It is not produced by external stimuli, resulting from condition within brain and sense organs. The subjective side of Truth means how much of the Truth, so refreshing in contemplation, is actually, by experience, ours. The subjective side of Truth is the realization of it; it has been personalized; it is experimental Truth vs. judicial or objective Truth.

OBJECTIVE—It is external; apart from self-consciousness; an end of action to be reached (not subjective). While contemplating, and meditating on Truth, we may be blessed and refreshed. This is the objective aspect of Truth, sometimes called judicial Truth. For example: Someone gives us a lovely statement of Truth which is purely objective; a little later God brings a little crisis, and says, "Now I am going to take that Truth, and make it a demonstration, (subjective realization) in your life.

Truth is never ours until it is personalized. It is never ours until we have laid ourselves open to God in our inner being, and the Spirit has been able to bring that Truth in, and we have, by faith, taken hold of it, and allowed that Truth to do the thing in us that it should. It may be creative, or perhaps corrective, but whichever it is, it is the material we will be using.

Truth is purely progressive in all forms. The heart has to be conditioned continually for its reception. It is an invisible miracle in the heart. Ten years from now it will have a fuller meaning.

There are fields of Truth not yet possessed. It takes a lifetime to have Truth converted in us.

All revelation, I don't care what field we may move in, is purely a progressive matter. It is eternally evolving; it is eternally moving. Why? Because it is inexhaustible. That is the center of all which is in God. God is infinite; Truth is infinite. Nobody can exhaust it. Nobody has a corner on Truth. It is just too big.

What you get out of a revelation is what you have brought to it. What we bring to Truth governs very much what we get out of it. Our testimony is what we have gotten out of the revelation. It will be governed by our own personal experience.

No conversations in the Word of God are accidental—not the words; nor the arrangement of the choice of words; nor their combination. That is what makes it so powerful.

Truth is very exacting and precise; it is settled forever. But the doctrines which we build on Truth may be very loose, and still be based on Truth. Truth comes by revelation; not by mental processes. I have tried that field of mental processes; I could define a lot of things, and analyze a lot of things; I know doctrine, and have taught it in college—that is fine intellectually, but that doesn't get us through. Truth comes by revelation. The mental processes are beautiful; wonderful; scholastic; intellectual; but we don't know God; we don't know Spirit; we don't know reality through that technique at all. It moves on a level here, and is good here; don't depreciate it; value it, but keep it in its place: on the level where God has placed it.

I can't make Truth. No one is original in that. God alone is its Author. But one may discover it, and it may become an obsession, or something of that nature. It is LIFE, and gives meaning to life. His will becomes the pattern, or design for living. The blessed Holy Spirit is Guide, and instructs, and furnishes the power, or dynamics for the out-working of His holy and precious purpose in the life of the one given to Him. In many ways it is like a dramatic adventure, full of heavenly interest, and material for the development of the new life in Him. So let us all move along patiently with Him. The agitated spirit only hinders. Faith is rest. But it is so difficult to reduce the natural man, and teach him to walk patiently with God.

After three years, Jesus could say, "Now are ye clean through the Word." The blood of Jesus will cleanse us from sin, but the power of the Word will cleanse us from all these strange, traditional things. There is a double cleansing continually. I have about nine places in the Word where Jesus washed his disciples from tradition by the Word.

Unless we learn to make a balance in the Truth, we will never have equipoise to stand in the Spirit.

The disciples were continually feeding themselves on one side of Truth, i.e. Christ in exaltation, but the other side of that Truth is Christ in humiliation.

Examples of the balance in Truth:

The brazen altar, and mercy seat were the same height.

Jesus fed four to five thousand, but could pick up the fragments.

There is a balance, an equipoise, in Truth. Properly, Truth has two legs:

1.   Right foot = Light and life—the positive teaching is of the Word of God, as victory, joy—it is creative.

2.   Left foot = Discipline, suffering, death—all the negative sides of the Truth—it is corrective.

Jacob's ladder was set on earth; angels ascending and descending. Why use a ladder? There are two sides of Truth. The ladder is not suspended from heaven. Its feet are attached to the earth.

There is no one original in Truth. Truth is quite original in itself. We don't make Truth; we discover it.

Truth only confirms; it never disturbs Truth. When an impact of Truth comes to you, it will never disturb, or dislodge anything that is Truth, but if there is something traditional, that becomes uneasy. If you have some things in there that are getting kind of jittery, something traditional, then that is disturbed. If it will upset anything, it won't be Truth that will be upset.

The Word of God is yet dead until the Spirit of God breathes Life through it. The letter of the Word is dead. The Word is Spirit and Life.

Discern the Truth, and live under the power of it. I think that is terrible not to be inwardly aroused to, what I call, the inner consciousness of Truth.

We can take a bit of Truth God gives us, and apply it over our initial, elementary experience in God, but, by and by, as we grow older, we can take that same Truth, and apply it over our lives, and we will find it will minister to us all over again. We have had this experience at one period in our lives, when he gave us a Scripture for our encouragement, strength, or vision, and maybe five years later when we read it, it ministers entirely differently to us. That is a sign we have been growing. Truth has that power; the application of the Word is repeated over and over—

here a little, and there a little; precept upon precept. It involves a process.

In our journey back to His loving heart, where we belong, He will have to use Truth over and over for our edification. Truth is corrective, but it is also illuminating; it has strange powers within us. Sometime it will bring a terrifying disappointment, but with it, a marvelous moving of the grace of God, so that in the end we would prefer the loss, the disappointment that we might have the grace which only comes through that method.

I can give you Truth in one lesson that will take a lifetime to work out.

I want you to find that He is adequate for your need, and I want you to have a fresh revelation of Him so that He might strengthen your capacity, and enlarge your powers of receptivity. This Truth has revolutionized my thinking, and, absolutely, my living. It has made an impact on me. The first reaction to Truth is devastating; the second is creative, and begins an illumination and a freedom and generosity in God which we are too cramped to receive at first. It takes great pressure to make capacity. This Truth will project itself to ages and ages. Why not pay a little bit now for a correct adjustment to God; correct adjustment to the things of God, so that when the time comes for our transition, we will not be too horribly surprised. We just can't go to glory—we have to be prepared.

I move in three realms continually: spiritual; soulish; physical—that's the way it should be; the way it was designed.

Our character is the sum total of our choices and decisions through life. When we hear Truth, it has made its impact; we cannot erase it.

Life will have some heartaches and headaches, but in God we have such wonderful victory. He is the Answer.

A mystery is a Truth that comes not by reasoning, but by revelation. It is not disclosed to us by a process of reasoning.

In the garden, Adam and Eve made girdles (aprons). What is your girdle as a Christian? It is the girdle of Truth. The earth is cursed today, and it cannot bring forth a thing that will make a girdle.

Anything new that denies the Truth which is given in the Bible, I have nothing to do with.

CHAPTER XLIII

TYPES

There are no non-essentials in God's Word. The Word is full of types, symbols, pictures; all have deep, peculiar, spiritual meaning.

The Tabernacle in the wilderness is a revelation of Truth—an object lesson of spiritual Truth. It is the revelation of Christ and His redemptive work; the story of the gospel. It teaches how God can meet His People, and how His people can come into the Presence of their God.

The first five books of the Bible are mostly types. Jesus is pictured as Lamb, Altar, Priest; varied glories of His Person, and varied aspects of His work. Jesus taught in types. The believer who has the most acquaintance with Jesus, who loves Him best, will see the most beauties in the types.

CHAPTER XLIV

VISION

The world is geared so that it wants everything done right now. But you can't do the work of God that way.

We need perspective in our thinking; in our studying; in our approach to God.

I am so thankful for what I call perspective in my vision of Truth. I know now His purpose, and only as I look away, and not too closely at the present, am I able to move on at all. "We look not at things seen." I must see them all in their logical purpose, but not park on anything too transitory.

We are all made to follow a vision of some sort, or pattern. All life and activity is due to motivation toward some desired end or purpose. What is our vision; or for what are we living? "Where there is no vision (no restraining power in life), the people cast off restraint." (Prov. 29:18)

CHAPTER XLV

WILL OF GOD

The highest expression of our spiritual life is, in the last analysis, back again to God. That is what we were made for. In the pattern and design for our living, God said He made us in His OWN IMAGE and LIKENESS. We were created for His glory and His pleasure—all things were created for this. We, the effect of His creation, ultimately, are unto the pleasure of God.

We were made to know the will of God, and to swing out in that norm. His will may take any pattern; plowing beans or potatoes, or preaching the gospel; it doesn't matter. The fact is, the soul has found an adjustment in God; embraces the will of God, and, if the will of God is for us to work on a farm, that is holy! Why? Because it is the farm? No. That work is a holy rendering because it is the will of God being performed. God is honored and blessed and glorified where His will finds expression. Wherever the will of God is being done, He is automatically glorified. "The heavens declare the glory of God." We get the benefit of the light and all that, but it was to the glory of God first.

When His will is executed, it is a reflection of His glory. This is true in the inanimate creation; in the mundane, the material world; wherever He produces a bit of His creative desire, it is always to His glory. Man's great objective, too, is to glorify God. How can we glorify God? By surrendering our will to His, and letting His will be wrought in us. Then we cannot help but glorify God.

Paul says, "I want to focus your thoughts, your prayers, your desires, every feature of your being, bound together in a strange cable toward one thing—glorifying God." God is setting before us an objective: "Whether therefore ye eat or drink or whatsoever ye do, do all . . ."—that ye might enter the pearly gates? No. That the kingdom of God shall come upon the earth? NO! "Do all to the glory of God!"

He never changed the objective for man. Man was made to glorify God and to give him pleasure. "And whatsoever ye do in word or deed, do all in the Name of the Lord Jesus, giving thanks to God . . ." (Col.

3:17) It all moves toward God. "If any man speak, let him speak as the oracles of God; if any man minister, let him do it as of the ability which God giveth; that God in all things may be glorified through Jesus Christ, to Whom be praise and dominion forever and ever, Amen." (1 Pet. 4:11) How do we glorify God? We can only glorify God by doing His will, and wherever the will of God is done, He is automatically glorified.

I have the joy of doing the will of God, but I don't always have the joy of doing the THING which is in the will of God.

In our life patterns, if we are dedicated spirits doing the will of God, He says, "I can make all these things work together for good, even the devil. Because I am God, and in My permissive will, I introduce all these foreign, strange elements. But I am God, and I can cause them to work together for good to you who are called by Me according to My purpose." What is His purpose? "For whom He did foreknow He also did predestinate to be conformed to the image of His Son that He may be the Firstborn among many brethren." (Rom. 8:29) Paul goes on to say, "Be not conformed to this world." (Rom 12:2) Don't be molded into the popular world mold; don't allow your life to be cast into that popular world mold, and become molded into a worldling, because that is a world mold. He says it will press. We know in the world they have a lot of troubles, but, you see, they don't let their troubles do them any good. It brings them to a place of defeat, and sometimes suicide.

When we do the will of God, we feed Him. "My meat and My drink is to do the will of God." (John 4:34) When did you feed Jesus last?

It always pleases me to see how God can work when we let Him do what He wants to do. He can establish a work; He can defend a work; and He can do anything He wants to, if we would only get in with His "want to", and not say, "Lord, I want to," but "Lord, what do You want to do?" Then we get through.

Most people think the will of God is the most superficial thing. Sometimes the will of God is so complicated, and intricate, and involved, that it takes prayer to get us in a place where we can receive, or even discern it. Paul found this so. (Col. 1:9-11) The will of God is the safest place in the world, but sometimes the most difficult.

God still sits on the throne. It is His world. He has a program. He has an infinite will that is pushing down through the centuries, and on over into the ages. How sweet and lovely when my little will, and your little will is swallowed up in that magnificent one of God!

The basic sin in all the world is self-will against the will of God. When we bring it down to its last analysis, it may take ten thousand forms; every sin that is committed is a form of self-will over against God's.

All of us have sinned, because we have not perfectly glorified God; all have missed the mark.

CHAPTER XLVI

WORD

Oh, the majestic, untouched will of God moving down through the ages! When we move in the will of God, it answers the thousands of questions we may ever have.

The most marvelous prayer we can ever pray is: "Have your way. Thy will be done. Speak, Lord, thy servant heareth Thee. Bring me the intimation; that Word; what is it You want?"—Walk that way. Learn to do that. It takes a little time, but it takes such a burden off us. Now, when He speaks that Word, it has all the authority of heaven back of it, and it has a creative power when He speaks it in our hearts. A grain of faith always comes with it. Our faith will lay hold of it, and we ought to have it, because we are obedient to a law.

Always be careful that the Word, the promise, the intimation which is governing you today, and you hold in confidence and faith, as a power for your prayer authority,—be sure that Word is something which God speaks, or brings to your heart, He may bring it to you by reading the Word; He may bring it through a message; He may bring it by literature; He may bring it by intimation of Spirit; He may bring it by speaking to your inner heart, even without words. He talks to me many times without words as I walk along with Him.

Never approach the Word as you would any other literature. The Holy Spirit is needed for its revelation. When we deal with the mysteries of God, don't expect to understand them with your natural mind; it is a divine thing. Come to the Word with:

1.   A clean heart

2.   An unbiased spirit,

3.   An open mind.

There is nothing casual in the Word. Everything in the Word is full of God; full of the Spirit and Life; every bit of it; it is not an accidental thing. It is perfectly designed, and purposely designed, but we read it so casually.

In the Old Testament, He gave us our letters. In the New Testament He puts them together, and, in the ages to come, we will read them.

You say you read the Word, but you sense something in it you have never really touched yet. You have gotten hold of the letter of the Word; you never yet have gotten hold of the fire, or the Spirit of it. You have to keep your spirit open, not your brains, to get the Spirit and Life of the Word.

As soon as the Spirit takes hold of the Word, He makes it a throbbing reality. The Word, through which Spirit and Life can vibrate and move, is the vehicle. The Word that Jesus brings is, in essence, Spirit and Life.

The Bible is the written letter of the Word, but Truth is tremendous. The Bible is the vehicle inspired of God; there is nothing in the world like it. No man could write it. It is divinely inspired. It is the instrument through which Life and Light vibrate. It is the Word of God, but Life moves through it. Life is not in this paper; it vibrates through it, through its message. We have to learn this. Keep your heart open. He is able to speak to you in a thousand ways, and a thousand tongues.

CHAPTER XLVII

WORSHIP

Isn't it nice when we do things in the Spirit without being told: "Now we will lift our hands etc. . ." No, lift them in the Spirit when He lifts them.

Worship isn't conducted by machinery; it is born of the Spirit. It is not mechanical, but uplifting, and ascending to God; to a holy God—holy, holy, holy—something fresh we offer from our hearts. If you don't have that kind of God, I'd trade Him off! He is white-heated holiness and purity—a fire that consumes. No flesh can stand in His Presence. "That no flesh should glory in His Presence." (I Cor. 1:29) These days this needs to be brought out and emphasized, because people try to pull Him down to their level. "Rejoice in the Lord ye righteous, and give thanks at the remembrance of His holiness." (Ps. 97:12)

Our highest vocation is not our ministry; it is adoration and worship. Man was made for the glory of God originally. Our attitude in God is what counts. Worship is a tremendous SELF-GIVING to God; something that comes from within, and is going right up to God; right back to God. We can't worship in ourselves. Worship is born of the Spirit. He can worship through us. We can't automatically worship. True worship is born of the Spirit.

There is a difference between praise and worship. Praise is something we do. Worship is of the Spirit. The nearer we come to Him, the more we feel like going down, down before Him; not this "Hello, Jesus" business, but like a dog by his master, who has such a sense of security and rest: "I just feel that I want to push up by You. You don't have to talk to me."

There are times, if the Lord could get certain spirits into a place of just worship and adoration; that would mean more to Him than a thousand things they could do. If we could just come into the swing of the Spirit that enters into worship; walk all day worshipping the Lord, while souls are going to hell? I tell you something; they went to hell before we were born, and will after we are gone. We get so entangled into these traditional patterns and things that we forget God. If God can be blessed and honored by being loved and worshiped all day, then love Him and worship Him all day!

You say, "We will have all the eternal ages in heaven to worship Him." You better practice a little down here. Get in tune with the Infinite, and learn the quietness of His heart. How far we are from this in so much we see and hear! When we get into God, we find He is just about a thousand miles away from so much stuff we have here, but that holds us; it fascinates us.

Churches in the book of Revelation have a work complex instead of a worship complex.

How many know when the judgment of God will be lifted off this earth, it will be like a great musical; a powerful instrument of praise. The morning stars will be singing together! Do trees sing? Yes, to a poet, and anyone in God, they do. The scientific approach to God is always so ghastly to me. They want God in capsule form, a prescription. He doesn't move that way; He is Spirit.

CHAPTER XLVIII

MISCELLANEOUS & GENERAL MAXIMS

Anything we hold and retain becomes a snare. The enemy came to Jesus, but had nothing to hang on to.

You can listen and not hear, and you can look, and not see! What do you see when you look?

Signs are for unbelievers to arouse them to a consciousness that there is something dramatic around. We, as believers, don't need an earthquake.

A mystic is one who has discovered a life in God—independent of his natural life. That is mystical, because it is above the natural.

The first place we find fear in the Bible is in Gen. 3:10. Fear doesn't belong in the vocabulary of a

Christian. It is a word that has been added to our vocabulary through sin and failure. Fear is the disorganizing element. The love of God is creative. "Perfect love casteth out fear." Love will beget and beget. When Peter walked on water—fear broke down the whole thing. Fear is always the disorganizing element in any field in God. "Fear hath torment", because it is the antithesis of love. Love is trust.

"For we know that all things work together for good . . ." (Rom. 8:28) He can make sickness, death, all things, even hell; He can make even the wrath of the devil to praise Him!

I am always afraid of the magnitude of a thing. He deals with a minority, a remnant, etc.

Things of the Spirit are mystically sweet.

Things of God in creation are silent, usually; filled with mystery; sweet.

Things of the enemy are most always destructive and noisy!

Satan is walking around seeking whom he may devour. The Lord is walking around finding somebody who would be interested in Him.

"God has made us what we are, creating us in Christ Jesus for the good deeds which are prepared beforehand by God as our sphere of action." (Eph. 2:10 Moffatt's Tr.)

In regard to dealing with a wayward minister, I feel I am not touching the Lord's anointed; I am correcting a piece of flesh!

The books of Revelation and Daniel are cryptic writings which take a peculiar, special adaptation for an interpretation in that field.

Duplicate idea: Jacob constrained the angel to bless him, and on the Emmaus Road, the disciples constrained Jesus to come in.

God's way:

(1) Opens prison door for Paul and Silas.

(2) Puts John on Patmos—not out.

One He delivers, the next one He doesn't—that's God's way.

"Two things have I required of Thee; deny me them not before I die: Remove far from me vanity and lies: give me neither poverty nor riches; feed me with food convenient for me: Lest I be full, and deny Thee, and say, Who is the Lord? Or lest I be poor, and steal and take the name of my God in vain." In other words: Deliver me from the abundance which would make me too independent, so I would forfeit my dependence. But don't let me be so starved that I can't live.

Never be afraid of your limitation, but don't try with all your might and main where it won't stretch. Give it to God. He can take a limitation, and make it to bless five thousand. That is the kind of God we have. Put your limitation of five loaves and two fishes into the hands of God, and say, "Oh, Lord, here it is."

Mary at Cana. (She is always present, and His disciples; she is always there!) Mary: "They have no wine." (John 2:1-4)—There is no "Mother" in Jesus' answer to her! He calls her: "woman"—flesh. She is an ambitious mother, patriotic, and defends the Lord, and tries to shine up His glory;—proving God!

Don't stand there to explain God, and defend God. We are not called to defend Him; we are called to worship God, and love Him. But it is so much easier to try to defend Him than it is to worship Him. It is so much easier to prove Him, than to walk with Him.

DAY: what does it mean in the Genesis creation? We get into trouble if we are not careful. The Hebrew word for "day" in Genesis is "Yom"—It really means an indefinite period of time. It does not set a time limit at all; it merely means a period. It may be twenty-four hours; a year; a thousand years. We say, "that day" meaning twenty-four hours. We cannot always do that in Bible study.

Once I had just a little wish; it made me think of David, when he was hunted as a partridge on a mountain, and he just gave a little expression of a secret wish, but God saw that secret wish in him which desired to have a drink of water from his own home well in Bethlehem. Soldiers heard it, endangered their lives, and went way back in there and got it. It broke David's heart; he didn't feel worthy even to drink it. He poured it out as a libation, giving it to God. "I am not even worthy to drink it." It was a fresh touch he had with God; a fresh avenue was opened. That is like these little wishes we have sometimes. God is interested in the most casual and unlikely incidents; in most incidental things which would pass almost unobserved. He is concerned with them, and causes the things to work together.

We are under a curse—God cursed the earth; "Cursed be the EARTH" for man's doings, and all the animals had to go into a subjection for which they were not accountable. I never go to a zoo, and see a poor lion, but I always feel apologetic. I say, "Poor thing; God never made you like that, never in the world; your ferocity; your ugliness; your blood thirst; all is a result of sin in the world.

God never created you to jump on something and kill it—never in the world." A curse—a judgment is upon ALL creation for man's sake.

"I have learned in whatsoever state I am, therewith to be content." Philippians 4:11 should read, "I have learned in whatsoever state I am to be independent of it—I have learned in any condition to be independent of it"—I will not allow it to harass me, torment me, or disturb me. I will gain out of it what God wants me to have, but I will be above it. I will in any kind of a condition be released from it.

Psychiatrists can pull it all apart, but they can't put it back together, because they have no kingpin. The Lord can put it together, because He is the greatest Psychiatrist, Psychoanalyst, and Psychologist in the universe. He can analyze us perfectly. He can take us all apart, and He can look step by step in every item in our beings. Then He says, "I can put you all together"—not around the ego, but around the Christ; not ego-centric—that would damage the whole thing—

but Christ-centered. He says, "Now let Me have all your faculties, and I will even put them together in the power of the Spirit, in a new-formed personality, in its correct shape."

He redeemed the nation Israel out of Egypt—a separation to God. The Red Sea opened to let them out of Egypt's power, and closed behind them to keep them out! As long as a man is governed by the world spirit, he can know but little of communion with God. "I will dwell in them" is closely followed by the precept, "Come out from among them and be ye separate." (2 Cor. 6:16, 17)

God spoke to Moses, and under the authority of God, the children of Israel could go right through the Red Sea, because they were in divine order, under a special word. The Egyptians "assayed" to do likewise. They saw how the Israelites got along beautifully, BUT they didn't have any "spoke". God had spoken to the Israelites—God had not spoken to the Egyptians. Therefore, they couldn't have the miracle, although they assayed to do likewise. They didn't have any Word from God. You have to have the Word from God for your authority. The Egyptians said, "Why, they went through, why can't we?" They tried it, and drowned!

Don't make things synonymous which are not synonymous, such as nature and character. The lovely new nature is a gift, but the character which He is after, is built. How? Through testing and proving. That is why gradation is all through the New Testament. Gradation is mentioned with regard to food, milk, meat, strong meat, and there is gradation when it speaks of babes, children, little children, grownup sons, fathers and mothers in Israel.

People right in this city can't be alone five minutes nor still five minutes. We've got to get a TV going, and a radio going, and a band going, and a hum dum going and a . . . . They live in that environment. Why? Because they would be scared to death to be five minutes in the Presence of God. There is no adjustment for them. They have become so exposed to these horrible things that they don't know what's the matter with them. So they take pills, and jump off bridges, and do anything.

The enemy cannot touch us as redeemed property, abiding in Him, walking consciously with God, only as God sees good. It was God Who gave the permission that Peter should be sifted. It was God Who gave the permission that Job should be tested. That was all under the permissive providence of God.

The devil hath desired . . . but God hath given him permission, the power, to test and prove them.

1 Cor. 1:30: "But of Him are ye in Christ Jesus, Who of God is made unto us wisdom, and righteousness, and sanctification, and redemption."— The Holy Spirit is seeking to conform us to His image. All the victories He won belong to me now because I am in Him. He is made unto me all that. So we don't have to struggle too hard.

"For with God nothing is ever impossible, and no Word from God shall be without power or impossible of fulfillment." (Luke 1:37 A.N.T.) We have to have the Word from Him first. Never take the initiative in moving into anything unless you have the Word of God to garrison you.

PRAYER

O, faith, thou glorious means of reaching, help us to see the desire and purpose of God. Teach us to relate in this Lazarus-hour of our experience—the tomb—to God's glory, and anoint our eyes to trace God's leading over the pressure, and through the distress until we may see God's glory.

GENERAL MAXIMS

If we know HIM, we know enough!

Christ's character is built in us; not given to us. Righteousness is imputed.

Never take the initiative in moving into anything unless you have the Word of God to garrison you. As soon as the Spirit takes hold of that Word, He makes it a throbbing reality.

The motto of Jesus' life: "I have come to do Thy will, O God."

Some leave the great essentials, and involve themselves with doctrinal issues.

Don't crowd God into two thousand years.

We were not made for the here and now; we were made for the heart of God.

The spiritual, mental and physical should all have their source in the Christ.

It is not a reformation, but a total deliverance when He comes.

When we move in the will of God, it answers about a thousand prayers.

There is such a difference between being religious and being spiritual.

Always watch out that you have not too many possessions. If you are not careful, those possessions will possess you!

Don't develop a devil consciousness; develop a God consciousness.

Too many are conscious of their limitations. Count HIM in! Remember what He did with five loaves and two fishes.

We should give to God our very best—and all that we have.

We can be just as holy, just as devoted to Jesus as we want to be; and we can walk just as near to Him as we want to.

We can let the hour of our visitation slip right away from us. Awareness—we have to be aware.

The highest vocation of any spiritual manifestation is worship and adoration; not service.

The whole issue between broken humanity and God is a question of life and death; not heaven and hell.

Lord, keep me alive until I die.

Humility is something which is birthed within, and, if we think we have it; we haven't!

In the realm of the Spirit, there is no distinction between secular and holy. Everything in God's sight, in this new life, is holy.

We learn the laws of living in the realm of spiritual reality by living.

"I don't want your gifts, your services, what you are doing; I want your HEART."

He has so many who serve Him, but so few who love Him!

Everybody wants the fruitage; nobody wants the death that causes the fruitage.

When He gives a word, it is creative, and has a measure of faith every time.

Miracles are for beginners, but, for disciples, He expounds all things.

Miracles appeal to the cosmic curiosity of the flesh. Don't commercialize them. Have spiritual adjustment in God. "Rejoice not in miracles, but that your name is written in heaven."

Many have the Christ, but they have not discovered the hidden treasures in Him. (Colossians 2:3)

Never "Why" God: Worship Him!

Truth is never ours until it is personalized in our lives.

It is good to have a disappointment once in a while. It will throw us into God like nothing else will.

He is always and forever the same, but He is seeking to change us.

You and I are basically made for His pleasure.

Don't read traditionally, or perfunctorily, because you think you have to read!

Just to please the heart of God one day at a time is wonderful. Don't let your life pattern project so far ahead that it swallows up the importance of the moment.

I like what I call an overall pattern and perspective in my thinking.

My ministry is only a means unto the end; it is not the end.

The instrument is always of greater value than what the instrument can do.

No experience, in itself, ever matures us.

The more we see and know Him: The more we love Him.

Anybody can stand a blessing, but few people can take a defeat, a disappointment.

Here (on earth) is the place of decision.

Then (in heaven) is the place of expression.

I am saved; I am being saved; I am yet to be saved.

Jesus said: "I made the testing; also a way of escape."

Everybody has enough entertainment; they need instruction!

God has all eternal ages to work out the problems that we can't work out here.

Every heart has its own discipline, its own cross, and its own dealings with God.

"Be still and know that I am God." Don't clatter so much!

My motto: Keep in the middle of the road.

We learn to pray by praying.

In a consecrated life, there are no accidents.

The martyrs in the arena in Rome had an inner life element: They had agape love. Some can't face a lion, because they cannot face themselves for five minutes!

The devil will tempt us with the identical setup God uses to test us. Temptation is always unto defeat and death. Testing is always unto strength and life.

A walk in the Spirit is not a gift; it is an attainment.

JOHN WRIGHT FOLLETTE

BIOGRAPHY

by

Carolyn Côté

ACKNOWLEDGMENTS

My writing of Follette's biography was aided by the following archivists, librarians, docents, professors, pastors and fans. The gracious help I received was not hard to come by and for that I am very grateful.

Nancy Brennan, Registrar General, National Huguenot Society, for your helpful referral to the great resources at Historic Huguenot Street.

Carrie Allmendinger, Archivist Librarian, Historic Huguenot Street, for your exceptional help researching the Follette family and pertinent photos.

The helpful staff at Taylor University Archives, for Follette's poem, *Harp of Friendship*, which was written while he was a student at Taylor and for the 1909 GEM yearbook page which lists Follette's course of study.

Carol A. Johnson, Coordinator, Haviland-Heidgerd Historical Collection, Elting Memorial Library, New Paltz, NY, for kindly providing the Freer House, fireside photo of Elizabeth Follette.

Glenn W. Gohr, Reference Archivist, Flower Pentecostal Heritage Center, for your generous help and for sending along several other references to Follette stored at FPHC.

Pam Crenshaw, Associate Professor, Archivist/Librarian, Vanguard University, for your patient help and generous research and discovery of previously unpublished photos of Follette.

Jennifer Palmentiero, Digital Services Librarian, Southeastern, NY Library, for your useful referral and Elizabeth Follette picture.

Burton K. Janes, adjunct seminary faculty, author of several books on Pentecostal church history, editor, ordained minister, for your generous, international loan of Elizabeth Baker's, *"Chronicles of a Faith Life."*

Kim Magnell, Archives Associate, Drew Theological Seminary, for your above and beyond research for any reference to Follette's junior year of theological study at Drew.

Rev. John R. Miller, Ph.D. (Regent University) Chief Academic Officer, Elim Bible Institute and College. Pastor of Education, Living Word Temple of Restoration, Rochester, NY, for your generous offering of the Follette section of your 2007 published work, *Contribution of the Duncan Sisters to the Pentecostal Movement.*

Timothy Cote, President, Two Trees Ministries, my dear husband, for your heartfelt and expert editing and support, thank you. May the Lord shower you with all His spiritual blessings in Christ Jesus.

John Wright Follette
Photo from Vanguard University Archives,
Costa Mesa, CA

Born October 30, 1883, in New Paltz, New York, John Wright Follette was an obedient servant of Jesus Christ. His obedience took several creative expressions: teacher, musician, singer, preacher, artist and poet. Though he never married or had children, he left the Body of Christ a living legacy of writing and preaching which continues to bear fruit in the hearts of believers.

During the early 1900's Follette was a recipient and an active participant in the outpourings of the Holy Spirit on both the east and west coasts of

America. He saw it all; he saw what served to mature believers and what served to stumble them. Later, his warnings regarding the wholesale claiming of Biblical promises and the seeking of signs and wonders were not well received in Pentecostal circles and he was often criticized. Time and experience proved him correct. Today, his works are a refreshing drink to disillusioned Pentecostals and busy but spiritually exhausted Christians all over the world.

Family

Follette's father, Hector T. Follette (also recorded as Follett, Foilett, and Fallet), was born to farmers Erastus and Lurancy Follett in 1853 in Roxbury, New York. Of English descent, Hector's ancestors first came to America from Dartmouth, England in the late 1600's.

Hector married Elizabeth Wright in 1877 and made a living as a teacher and farmer. Later, he was known as a respectable salesman in the grocery business. He died in New Paltz, New York in 1915 when John was 32. (Elizabeth died in 1945 when John was 62).

Follette's mother, Elizabeth (also recorded as Liza and Lyzie) Wright was born in 1859 in Accord, New York. Of French Protestant (Huguenot) descent,

Elizabeth Follette's ancestor, Hugo Frere (later spelled Freer), fled from France to Mannheim, Germany in 1651 due to the great persecution of the Huguenots. In 1660, while in Germany, Freer married Marie De La Haye and by 1666 the couple had two daughters and one son also named Hugo. In 1667, though baby Hugo was spared, Marie and both daughters died, likely from bubonic plague. That same year, Freer remarried the widow Janettje Wibau Floquete and in the 1670's the family joined a company of Huguenots who immigrated to America in 1675. In 1677, this company of twelve families were given a patent by British Governor Edmond Andros to purchase 40,000 acres in the Hudson River Valley in New York. The tract, originally purchased from the Esopus Indians, was newly named New Paltz and the patentees' settlement was built on the Walkill River. In 1683, the small company formed their first church and appointed Freer a deacon. In 1690, he was appointed to an eldership. Janettje Wibau Freer died December 8, 1693 and Hugo Freer died in 1698. Both are buried in the Huguenot Cemetery at New Paltz, New York.

Hector and Elizabeth Follette had four children: Eva (1878-1947), Mabel (1881-1907), John (1883-1966) and Mary (1886-unkown). John Wright Follette and his three sisters were among the eighth generation of descendants born of Hugo Freer.

When John was born, Hector and Elizabeth originally named him Levi to honor his maternal grandfather but upon hearing the news Levi Wright opposed the honor saying, "I have suffered under that name; don't do it." Levi was renamed John.

It appears John was raised by his mother with a profound awareness and appreciation for his Huguenot ancestors and he and his sisters where raised in the Protestant faith. New Paltz Methodist Church records indicate that John and two of his three sisters, Mabel and Mary, were baptized December 25, 1887 and his parents became members of that church in 1888.

Follette was forever grateful for his upbringing. His family's farm provided exposure to the natural realm which Follette said allowed several spiritual truths to inform his growing faith. One such truth he referenced was how his summers were spent shoeless allowing him to walk barefoot in the furrows of freshly plowed soil. This experience later helped him understand the necessity of the hard ground of the soul to be plowed if spiritual truth is to take root and mature.

Education

The source of Follette's primary education is unclear but later he was schooled at the New York Normal School in New Paltz, which offered high school, teacher training and college level instruction.

The New Paltz Normal School in the late 1800s. The school was destroyed by fire in 1906. Haviland-Heidgerd Historical Collection. Photo by Erma Dewitt.

In 1907, Follette travelled eighty miles to study for the ministry at Drew Theological Seminary of the Methodist Episcopal Church. In a message Follette preached when he was seventy-five, he described that during this time, his first away from home, he suffered a horrible night of consecration where all his earthly affections, including his attachments to family, went to the cross. Suffering the sacrifice, he grieved as though his family had all died. The Lord asked him, "Will you fall into my hands? All I want is to possess you."

Follette answered the call and assented to give the Lord his full devotion. This would soon be tested when on November 5, 1907, John received word by telegram of his sister's sudden death from pregnancy complications. Mabel Follette Dubois, age 27, was survived by her husband and a premature son. Sadly, the baby died a few days later. Follette returned home for the burial and as he paid his last respects at the viewing he broke into songs of praise to God causing the undertaker to be confused about how to comfort him.

From 1908-1909, Follette studied at Taylor University. The Register for 1908 lists him as a junior in Philosophical Studies.

In 1910, Follette took a short-term pastorate in Geneseo, N.Y.

About this time, the Duncan sisters of Rochester, N.Y., began a ministry that would forever change the direction of Follette's life. Over a three-decade period beginning in 1895, the five Methodist sisters, led by the eldest, Elizabeth Baker, became the founders of

Elim Faith Home, Elim Publishing House, Elim Tabernacle Church and Rochester Bible Training School. During a convention the sisters hosted in 1907, prayers for an outpouring of the Holy Spirit as had been experienced on the other side of the country (Azusa Street) were answered by a Pentecostal outpouring of signs and wonders. This led to the opening of Rochester Bible Training School (RBTS), the first permanent Bible school to train charismatic men and women in the 20th century. John Wright Follette entered this school in 1910 and was ordained by the Council of Pentecostal Ministers at Elim in 1911.

While still a student, Follette had an experience so remarkable it was included in Elizabeth Baker's autobiography, *Chronicles of a Faith Life*, which was published after her death in 1915:

> The most convincing incident occurred in our midst one Sabbath evening which proved three things, viz., that a real tongue was spoken, that the correct interpretation was given, and that the manifestation was edifying.
> The service opened with singing of hymns and the Spirit at once began to move upon us, so that several were worshipping in the new tongue, some praying audibly and some breaking forth to speak with great

feeling and power in the new tongue. As he (Follette) went on for some time, Mrs. Baker, who was seated on the platform, arose and said, "He is giving the scene of the nativity, describing the star in the East, the angelic messengers, and the birth of Christ, and the humiliation of the god-head in the incarnation." Although Mr. Follette was unable to speak in English, as this interpretation was given, he signified by gesture that it was correct. After this he burst forth in song, which was most beautiful and impressive. When he had ceased, the service went on and a sermon was delivered.

At the close of the service a lady and gentleman who were present, called one of the sisters aside and asked, "Who was that young Jew who spoke and sang tonight?" They were told that there was no Jew present, but that it was one of the students. With great surprise the gentleman informed us that he and his wife had been residents of Paris, France, for several years, and that he understood several languages, among them the Hebrew, and, said he, "The young man spoke and sang in the most perfect Hebrew, and we understood every word he was saying, and the interpretation given was correct." He then said that the singing was the absolutely perfect rendering of a Psalm, which he had heard many times in the Synagogues in Paris, and added, "It was a favorite of Queen Victoria, who listened to it upon every possible occasion." He also said that the rendition of the melody was impossible to an American, and added, "I would compliment you if it had been your own effort, but I accept your explanation that it must have been the Spirit of God." He declared that the Hebrew and the melody, with every intonation and variety of expression was unique and could not be reproduced by a foreigner except in this supernatural manner.

Teaching Ministry

Soon after Follette's 1911 ordination, he began to serve at RBTS as a teacher and minister and would remain on staff until 1921. Students came to RBTS from Methodist churches all over the United States to prepare for ministry and for the foreign mission field. Follette taught Bible and music classes and is often seen in RBTS group pictures standing tall, lean and solemn.

Rochester Bible Training School, Rochester New York, Photo from Flower Pentecostal Heritage Center.

Follette with, from left, Mary Duncan Work, Susan Duncan, and Harriet (Hattie) Duncan. Photo from Flower Pentecostal Heritage Center.

Follette with Harriet (Hattie) and Susan Duncan. Photo from Flower Pentecostal Heritage Center.

Follette, far right, with students at Rochester Bible Training School in 1917. Photo from Flower Pentecostal Heritage Center.

In 1915, Follette's father died in New Paltz, N.Y.

In 1918, at age 34, Follette's draft card issued in Rochester, N.Y., lists his occupation as "Minister," his eye color "brown," and his frame and build as "medium and slender."

In 1919, Follette wanted to bless his RBTS students with a gift. Without the resources to buy gifts he was at a loss until the idea came to him to write them a poem about the birth of Christ. Thus began an annual tradition which spanned over forty years (1919-1965). The forty poems, each centered on the incarnation of Christ, were written from different perspectives and each served to teach using allegory the mysteries of following Christ. The poems have since been published under the title, A *Christmas Wreath.*

In 1921, at age 38, Follette left RTBS and crossed the country to take a teaching position at the newly formed Southern California Bible School. SCBS classes were held at the spacious, donated home of Rev. and Mrs. Harold K. Needham on Echo Street in Los Angeles. Beginning with twenty students, a year later, there were over thirty five and the growth continued.

Follette at his living quarters as dean at Southern California Bible College. Vanguard University Archives, Costa Mesa, CA.

The decision to hire Follette is described in the 1923-24 SCBS yearbook:

> At the close of the second year, with the call of Brother Kerr and Peirce from our staff of instructors to Bible school work in the Middle West, we felt the Lord beginning to move in different directions to bring in others

who might take up the work where they left off . After much prayer and waiting upon God, and the evidence that it was His hand that was leading, arrangements were made with Rev. John W. Follette, for thirteen years connected with the Rochester Bible Training School of Rochester, N. Y., to take up the work with us as teacher in Bible Doctrine, Homiletics and Dispensational Studies of the Bible. In response to the call, Brother Follette joined the corps of teachers and has proved through the past year his ability in faithfully opening the Scriptures in not only an intelligent and clear interpretation, but from a spiritual standpoint his work is particularly inspiring."

Follette is also mentioned in a book about the school's history by Lewis Wilson, A Vine of His Own Planting:

> John Wright Follette, one of the most popular and influential teachers in the school's history, lived in the rustic cottage and two future missionaries, George Carmichael and Irvin Bullard, slept in a tent at the rear of the property. Kerr's son-in-law, Willard Peirce,

served as the first dean followed by John Wright Follette, and Frank Boyd. All were talented teachers, writers, and conference speakers.

Follette, near center, with a SCBS graduating class, Photo from Vanguard University Archives, Costa Mesa, CA.

Elizabeth Follette moved from New York to join her son at SCBS in 1923 and was remembered as a great asset to the student body.

About the time Follette decided to move on to other endeavors, the growing school purchased a five acre campus in Pasadena but later would move further south to Costa Mesa to become the present day Vanguard University.

In 1928, Follette, along with his mother, left SCBS and made his way back to New Paltz, N.Y., by way of Colorado Springs, CO., where he spent 1928-1930.

Travel

Follette became officially affiliated with the Assemblies of God in 1935 and the network of contacts within the organization soon drew on Follette's spiritual insight and maturity as a teacher and conference speaker. This new season of international travel took Follette around the world. The first leg of the journey was a long steamship trip to Australia and Follette was terrified at the prospect due to his propensity to seasickness. Follette took his fears to the Lord and in an act of pure obedience he told the Lord he would submit to the ocean voyage and inevitable sickness with the hope that maybe a steward would come to the Lord through it. Miraculously, when most everyone else became sick, Follette only became sleepy and was able to sleep away the hours as the ship rolled.

In 1943, Follette had an unusual opportunity to purchase from Margaret A. Mamions his 250 year old ancestral home on Huguenot Street in New Paltz.

Over the next twelve years, Follette and his mother modernized (central heat, plumbing and electricity) and restored the old stone house. After Follette's mother died in 1945, Follette lived alone and continued the work. In 1955, Follette sold the home to the Huguenot Society which provides tours to this day.

Freer House during the time of Follette's ownership. Photo from *The Street of the Huguenots* by Kenneth E. Hasbrouck and Erma R. DeWitt, 1952.

Follette's mother, Elizabeth Follette, enjoying her renovated and restored ancestral home (the Freer House) in New Paltz, N.Y., Photo from Haviland-Heidgerd Historical Collection, Photo by Erma Dewitt

Freer House as it appears today.

In his seventies and eighties, Follette was called upon to teach at small retreats of believers he knew from his former years of teaching. He used those opportunities to share more personal experiences from his youth including the unusual affect that certain sounds had on him. At one such retreat, he shared that, as a youngster, the evening sound of the Whip-poor-will bird bothered him so much that he would hide under his parent's bed and weep. As an adult he detailed this experience in his poem, "To a Wood Thrush." Also affecting him with a distracting sense of restlessness was the sound of crashing waves to the point that he once had to shorten a vacation to the coast. Some sounds were, to him, accompanied by visual washes of abstract art. He knew he wasn't crazy, and indeed today's physician would tell him he had the creative gift of synesthesia.

Follette went home to be with the Lord on October 3, 1966 in New Paltz from complications of a stroke. Jay Hearn (archive.org) reports that Hattie Hammond, a co-laborer of Follette's was present at his passing. She testified that as Follette was passing he experienced heavenly visions, unnerving the nursing staff. "As his spirit was leaving his body" Hattie said, "he was physically lifted above the bed until his passing. There was such a presence of the Lord in his room!"

John Wright Follette, Photo from Flower Pentecostal Heritage Center

Writing Ministry

Books and pamphlets written by Follette:

1936, Smoking Flax and Other Poems

1942, Fruit of the Land

1957, Broken Bread

Published Posthumously:

1968, A Christmas Wreath

1969 Arrow of Truth, Sermons and Poems

1973 The Three-Fold Witness of God

1974 This Wonderful Venture Called Christian Living

1978 Paul's Sevenfold Vision and Method of Attainment

1980? The Costly Quest

1985 Golden Grain

1989 Gideon

1994 Pressed Juice from Living Fruit

Made in the USA
Charleston, SC
02 September 2015